NEW FEDERALIST PAPERS

NEW FEDERALIST PAPERS

Essays in Defense of the Constitution

ALAN BRINKLEY

NELSON W. POLSBY

KATHLEEN M. SULLIVAN

A TWENTIETH CENTURY FUND BOOK

W. W. NORTON & COMPANY ◆ NEW YORK ◆ LONDON

The Twentieth Century Fund sponsors and supervises timely analyses of economic policy, foreign affairs, and domestic political issues. Not-for-profit and nonpartisan, the Fund was founded in 1919 and endowed by Edward A. Filene.

Library of Congress Cataloging-in-Publication Data

Brinkley, Alan
  The new Federalist papers : essays / Alan Brinkley, Nelson W. Polsby, and Kathleen M. Sullivan.
   p. cm.
  "A Twentieth Century Fund book."
  ISBN 0–393–04619–2
  1. Democracy--United States. 2. Representative government and representation--United States. 3. Untied States--Politics and government--1989- I. Polsby, Nelson W. II. Sullivan, Kathleen M. Ph. D. III. Title.
JK1726.B75 1997
324' .0973--dc21
                  96-48355
                  CIP

Cover Design, Illustration, and Graphics: Claude Goodwin
Manufactured in the United States of America.

10 9 8 7 6 5 4 3 2 1

PREFACE

Our nation's history reflects a deep mistrust of central authority—the original framework for the newly independent nation embodied in the Articles of Confederation was not weak by accident. In 1787, despite the clear inadequacy of the Articles, the strong, representative national government championed by the framers of the Constitution was a hard sell. The founders themselves disagreed sharply and fundamentally about the right mix of Athenian assembly and Roman senate for America. But most put aside their differences to fight for the ratification of the Constitution. They succeeded, in part because they made the case that a representative federal republic was preferable to a more direct and decentralized version of democracy.

The debate about our system of governance, however, has never ended. One hundred years ago, William Jennings Bryan and others—feeding off the discontent caused by declining farm prices, discriminatory commercial practices, and industrial dislocations—revived one side of the old argument in a new form called populism. Outraged at the power of big business and its influence over government, they sought to check the "ascendancy of capital" through changes in policy and structure that would put the government squarely on the side of the average citizen.

Today, in modern dress, one can discern a somewhat similar challenge to the status quo. Indeed, it would be surprising if wrenching, contemporary changes in politics, industry, families, and culture had not produced a strong reaction. Today's new movement is at once radical and conservative—anxious for sweeping change and nostalgic for a half-imagined past. Central to the movement is the belief that government is inaccessible, unresponsive, and unworkable; that it seldom, if ever, has the potential to be reformed into an ally. While populism looked to government to remedy the failures of the marketplace, the radical-conservatives revel in unfettered markets. In those limited portions of the public sphere that they see as absolutely necessary, they advocate sweeping devolution of responsibilities from the national government to the states.

At its most extreme, the current assault on government—on the federal government in particular—threatens domestic tranquillity. It has spawned a grotesque collection of armed militia, nativist bigots, and even mad bombers. (Some, oddly, believe that in the midst of government gridlock, we are on the verge of dictatorship.) Government, much of the right claims, is a conspiracy against the people. This perception lies behind the ravings of some right-wing radio talk show hosts; it is common fare in our popular culture, especially in movies and television. On the big screen, the solution is all too often: don't throw the bums out, blow them away. In the real world, public services are among the first casualties in the war against government, and there is "collateral damage" to those who depend on the public sector for schooling, food, shelter, medical care, and protection. To the zealots, this is a small price to pay for reestablishing "American values."

Much of the disaffected mainstream of the new movement is especially entranced with the presumed tonic effects of more direct democracy. The movement into the cybernetic age makes "interactivity" easier than ever before. Reform proposals often marry a high-tech twist to a low regard for authority. Televised "town halls," electronic plebiscites, instant polling, and "third wave" breakthroughs in technology are touted as means of "empowering" the people. This surge toward direct democracy is also evident in the growth of ballot initiatives and referenda, as well as in proposals for national plebiscites. And support for term limits is strong almost everywhere outside of Washington.

The assault on government threatens the fundamentals of the American system; it has taken formal shape in a host of legislative initiatives and hundreds of proposed amendments to the Constitution. What is perhaps most remarkable is the fact that so many amendments are being given serious consideration in Congress. Amendments relating to balanced budgets, flag desecration, super-majorities for taxes, and the line-item veto are only suggestive of the range of topics addressed by those who seek to reshape the constitutional order. If many are adopted, the impact on the Constitution, as we know it, would be profound. All this is occurring even though the nation is at peace and generally enjoying prosperity.

Surely, the time has come for reconsideration. We need a powerful reminder that constitutional amendments should be rare and limited to issues of historic significance. Our basic governmental structure, after all, has stood the test of time, usually achieving consensus despite the complexity of our democracy; indeed, the Great Republic has earned global envy for providing the best mix of liberty, community, and abundance.

A century ago, populism's surge provoked an important bipartisan movement that elevated public debate and ultimately trumped simplistic solutions by offering meaningful reform. The result was a progressive agenda that tamed the trusts, regulated the banking system, preserved national forests, and offered professionalism in government. Today, the task of constructive reform is, if anything, more complicated: to preserve the Constitution from the short-term and self-interested passions and to sustain the social safety net in face of a new Social Darwinism. The starting point once again is to teach the merits of representation, deliberation, and conciliation.

The general public, on the evidence of the past two national elections, is ambivalent. Voters say that they favor change, but they are not clear about either the amount of change they want or the direction it should take. Conventional political debate has done remarkably little to enhance public understanding of the underlying constitutional issues. But there is still time for those who treasure America's unique governmental structure to speak up. More serious discussion is not only overdue; it is a practical necessity. For one thing is certain: the greatest threats to constitutional government spring from the paucity of serious public discourse, and thus from an uninformed public.

Over the years, the Twentieth Century Fund has examined many aspects of the federal system. Currently, we are coproducing a series of television programs ("The Fred Friendly Seminars") that explore the debate about American government; and we are publishing studies that examine proposals to restructure the roles of the states and the national government.

This volume occupies a special place in our program. We asked three eminent scholars to respond to the contemporary attack on the Constitution by writing essays reframing the arguments for the basic structure of the American government. Alan Brinkley, professor of history at Columbia University; Nelson W. Polsby, professor of political science at the University of California, Berkeley; and Kathleen M. Sullivan, professor of law at Stanford University, responded with insight and wisdom to our request. As planned, each essay is written to stand on its own. Some already have appeared in newspapers and periodicals. Taken together, they form an important contribution to the national debate about the future of the Republic.

The founders did not choose our system by accident. These New Federalist Papers are intended as a challenge to those who would dismantle it by design. On behalf of the Trustees of the Twentieth Century Fund, I thank Alan Brinkley, Nelson W. Polsby, and Kathleen M. Sullivan for their contributions.

RICHARD C. LEONE, PRESIDENT
The Twentieth Century Fund
New York, 1997

CONTENTS

Preface by Richard C. Leone   v

Introduction   1

PART 1: THE FORESIGHT OF THE FRAMERS

Chapter 1. The Contemporary Relevance of
The Federalist by Kathleen M. Sullivan   7

Chapter 2. The Assault on Government
by Alan Brinkley   15

Chapter 3. The Challenge to Deliberative
Democracy *by Alan Brinkley*   23

Chapter 4. On the Distinctiveness of the American
Political System *by Nelson W. Polsby*   29

PART 2: MODERN POLITICS AND ITS DISCONTENTS

Chapter 5. The American Party System
by Nelson W. Polsby   37

Chapter 6. The Presidential Campaign, British
Style *by Nelson W. Polsby*   45

Chapter 7. Money in Presidential Campaigns
by Nelson W. Polsby   51

Chapter 8. Campaign Finance Reform: A Response to
Nelson W. Polsby *by Alan Brinkley*   55

PART 3: THE CONSTITUTION IN A WORD PROCESSOR

Chapter 9. What's Wrong with Constitutional
        Amendments? *by Kathleen M. Sullivan*   61

Chapter 10. Term Limits *by Nelson W. Polsby*   69

Chapter 11. Democracy and the Federal Budget
        by Kathleen M. Sullivan   75

Chapter 12. The Item Veto *by Nelson W. Polsby*   81

PART 4: DELICATE BALANCES

Chapter 13. Liberty and Community
        by Alan Brinkley   87

Chapter 14. Representation of Racial Minorities
        by Kathleen M. Sullivan   103

Chapter 15. The Balance of Power between the
        Federal Government and the States
        by Kathleen M. Sullivan   111

Chapter 16. Relegitimizing Government
        by Alan Brinkley   123

PART 5: THE NEXT MILLENNIUM

Chapter 17. The Privatization of Public
        Discourse *by Alan Brinkley*   139

Chapter 18. The Role of the Media in Represen-
        tative Government *by Kathleen M. Sullivan*   151

Chapter 19. Constitutional Angst: Does American
        Democracy Work? *by Nelson W. Polsby*   159

INTRODUCTION

In the aftermath of the Constitutional Convention of 1787, a great debate emerged in the young American republic between those who supported the new plan for a national government and those who opposed it—a debate between two groups known to history as the federalists, who supported the Constitution, and the antifederalists, who opposed it. That debate raged for months not only in state conventions deciding whether or not to ratify the Constitution but also in taverns and churches, at town halls and mass meetings, in the columns of newspapers, and in ordinary conversation. At times, passions became so intense that they produced violence and at least once (in Albany, New York) death.

Opponents considered the Constitution a betrayal of the principles of the American Revolution, a vehicle for establishing a tyrannical center of power. The antifederalists were not anarchists, of course. But they were much more afraid of a strong national government than they were of the states or the people, and they opposed the Constitution because it quite deliberately created a buffer between popular will and the exercise of public power, because it was a design not for a "pure" or direct democracy but for a republic—that is, a representative democracy.

To answer the antifederalists, three of the most gifted participants in the Constitutional Convention—Alexander Hamilton, James Madison, and John Jay—wrote a series of eighty-five essays, widely published in newspapers throughout the nation, defending the proposed new government against its detractors. Those essays, known today as the "Federalist Papers," constitute America's most important contribution to political theory. They explain the philosophical basis of the Constitution, defend the idea of republican government against charges that it would lead to tyranny, and suggest the dangers of a decentralized political system in which popular passions and local or private interests remain unchecked, in which the national government would be incapable of representing the national interest.

The framers of the Constitution wanted a national government strong enough to preserve the fragile Union and promote the general welfare. Like the antifederalists, they feared excessive centralized power. But they feared inadequate national power even more, convinced that without it there would be no protection against chaos and disunion. They were, after all, creating a government to replace the highly decentralized system set up under the Articles of Confederation, which they considered inadequate to the nation's needs. The Constitution was, therefore, an effort to strengthen, not to limit, what we now call the federal government.

The political controversies of our own time are neither so fundamental nor profound as those of the 1780s. But they do call into question some of the principles that have shaped government and politics as we have known them through much of this century, and indeed through most of our national history. The essays published here, inspired in part by the spirit of the original Federalist Papers, are an effort to stimulate public debate on some of the issues now before us.

Like the original federalists, we are defenders of a strong and vigorous national government, although we are skeptical of many aspects of politics and government in their present form. Like the federalists, we see substantial danger in the current effort to diminish and relocate federal power, although we recognize the importance of state and local governments, of market forces, and of the many other intermediate institutions on which a healthy society depends.

It is, we realize, extraordinarily presumptuous to present a series of essays as a "New Federalist Papers." We do so not because we expect to match the intellectual or literary power, or the impact, of the originals. Clearly we will not. We do so because we believe, as the federalists believed, that much is at stake in the public issues of our time and that it is the task of public discourse to bring about a reasoned consideration of those issues. These essays are meant as a small contribution to that task.

Part 1

The Foresight of the Framers

Chapter

1

THE CONTEMPORARY RELEVANCE OF *THE FEDERALIST*

by Kathleen M. Sullivan

The framers of the Constitution empowered the federal government in the belief that it was the best check we have on the "propensity of mankind to fall into mutual animosities," as James Madison wrote in *The Federalist* No. 10. Yet many contemporary critics of the federal government urge that federal powers be devolved to the states. With such a massive power transfer, welfare, health care, environmental, and other policies would be governed not in Washington but rather in fifty separate statehouses. Much attention has been focused on what effects this would have on particular programs. More should be focused on how it would dismantle the basic premises of our nation's founding.

The framers of the federal government had a number of goals in mind when they drafted the Constitution and urged its ratification upon the states. They sought to fashion a unified national government strong enough to defend the nation against foreign enemies and to prevent conflict across state lines. They aimed at creating a national market in which goods and labor could flow freely in interstate commerce. But by empowering the federal government, they sought above all to solve what Madison called the problem of "faction." The divisive forces of passion and interest, they believed, would inevitably plague government on the small scale of the states. Extend the sphere of government to national dimensions, however, and such destructive factionalism could be kept in check.

To understand this requires recalling the theory Madison set forth in *The Federalist* No. 10. The framers believed the tendency toward faction to be sown in human nature: "the propensity of mankind to fall into mutual animosities" disposes us more "to vex and oppress each other than to cooperate for the common good." Some factions arise from passion—the opinion that one is right and others wrong on matters of politics or of faith. Think of current divisions over abortion or affirmative action or gay service members in the military. Others arise from economic interest—"the most common and durable source of factions has been the various and unequal distribution of property." Consider current struggles over tax cuts or deregulation or access to medical care. The only way to prevent factions is to cut off political liberty—a cure far worse than the disease. Yet no popular democracy can endure, warned Madison, unless it can find some way to "break and control the violence of faction."

The framers' ingenious and so far enduring solution to the problem of faction was one of institutional design: build a strong federal government that would combine the twin virtues of indirect democracy and the extended sphere. In Madison's view, factions always dominate in a small, direct democracy run by popular vote, causing discord and oppression. The remedy? To "refine and enlarge the public views by passing them through the medium of a chosen body of citizens" elected by the rest. How to guard against the election of representatives with their own "fractious tempers"? Choose "an extensive republic" over government on a state or local scale, Madison advised. The smaller the government, the more homogeneous. Thus, state and local governments are vulnerable to factional capture. "Extend the sphere" of government to the federal level, however, "and you take in a greater variety of parties and interests," far more politically, socially, and religiously diverse than those of any state. This, Madison wrote, creates "greater security, afforded by a greater variety of parties, against the event of any one party being able to outnumber and oppress the rest."

On the framers' theory, a massive decentralization of power is exactly the wrong prescription for a time when passions run high and interests are in sharp competition. No one can doubt that the late twentieth century, no less than the late eighteenth, is such a time. Real incomes have stagnated, and the wealth gap has widened. "Angry white men" decry governmental preferences for minorities and women. Longtime residents blame immigrants for taking jobs and public services. Antigovernment "militias" organize to resist federal agents. And talk radio and the Internet fuel such passions with a speed never known before. The solution to these divisions is *not* to dismantle the federal government—the only device anyone has come up with in our political history for keeping factionalism under control.

Some critics of the federal government suggest that the conditions necessary for the federal government to control factionalism have disappeared in modern life. Madison envisioned that national representatives would distance themselves and be detached from popular sentiment in their deliberation about the public good. But electronic polling today conveys to politicians every ripple of public feeling. And continuous C-SPAN coverage and twenty-four-hour news services expose every move of members of Congress instantly to their constituents. These are the conditions of reactive, not deliberative, democracy, the skeptics charge. Madison also envisioned that it would be more costly and difficult for factions to mobilize at the national than at the state and local level. But today, note the critics, technological advances in communication and transportation make factions' access to the nation's capital quite cheap. So much for Madison's prediction that minority factions would be unable "to discover their own strength and to act in unison with each other" at the national level. Finally, say the doubters, Madison envisioned a limited federal government that would offer factions little in the way of spoils. But the Sixteenth Amendment has since given Congress the power of progressive income taxation, and with it the power to fashion federal agencies and programs on a scale unimagined by the framers. Thus, factions have greater incentives today to promote their passions and interests at the federal level. This potent combination of means and motive, critics argue, has created a crisis of federal government by special interest—a crisis they predict will somehow be solved by casting off large chunks of federal power to the states.

These new antifederalists are wrong. First, they ignore our history. While it is true that much has changed since Madison's time, history has, if anything, proved Madison right about the crucial role of the federal government in constraining faction. Second, they greatly overrate the virtues of contemporary states—indeed, so much so that they might be suspected of other motives.

To begin with, consider the two principal episodes of federalization of power that have taken place since the nation's founding. The first was Reconstruction, following a bloody civil war in which the national government broke the local grip of the slaveholding faction. The Reconstruction amendments to the Constitution, which abolished slavery and gave African-Americans rights of equal citizenship, set the stage for the civil rights victories of the 1950s and 1960s. It took all three branches of the federal government to eliminate state and local tyranny of the majority based on race: the federal courts mandated desegregation, but federal troops and congressional civil rights acts were needed to back them up. In matters of race, then, only the federal government could control oppressive localism and prove, in Madison's words, "superior to local prejudices and to schemes of injustice."

Federal power was consolidated a second time with the New Deal. Again, federal programs supplied the answer to problems that proved intractable at the level of the states—this time because capital and labor can move freely across state lines. States' rights advocates have always celebrated that mobility. They argue that it permits a healthy competition among the states to attract businesses and citizens, who in turn vote with their feet for the public policies they like. But there is a dark side to interstate mobility, as the Great Depression made quite clear. No state wants to be the first to adopt Social Security or abolish child labor unless other states will do the same. Any one state enacting progressive reforms risks losing business and thus revenue to others, setting off a race to the bottom among the states. The great insight of the New Deal was that the federal government could stop such destructive behavior by imposing redistributive measures uniformly nationwide.

While forgetting these lessons of history, current critics of the federal government also romanticize the states as being much closer to the people. They portray the states as fountainheads of participatory democracy, of popular rule by ordinary citizens. This portrait is inaccurate. Most states are themselves too big in size and population to permit genuine participatory democracy. When the states do practice direct democracy, it is fueled by passion and interest, not reason and deliberation, just as Madison predicted. Consider California, a state in which legislation is frequently proposed directly on the ballot by initiative and referendum. Many such ballot measures have arisen in groundswells of passion. One such measure denied most public services to illegal aliens and their children, and another repealed all voluntary public affirmative action measures. Many other ballot measures have been the efforts of organized economic interest groups. While the initiative and referendum were invented by progressives as vehicles for returning power to the people, they are often today the tools of powerful corporations instead. Turning a citizen's trip to the ballot box into a mini-legislative session is likely to promote voter confusion or indifference, or to give the victory on ballot measures to the side that spends the most on advertising.

Nor does the smaller scale of the states create significant advantages. Constituents scarcely have greater ties of familiarity and affection to their state representatives than to their representatives in Congress. And, like the federal government, most states have developed elaborate permanent bureaucracies. Thus, most citizens participate directly in government only at the local level, if at all. But it is at the local level that the problem of faction is most acute. Madison warned of the tyranny of local majorities, observing that the "malady" of faction "is more likely to taint a particular county or district than an entire State." But in today's political atmosphere, local governments can also be captured by well-organized minority factions, a problem Madison did not foresee. Minority interests flourish in an atmosphere of voter cynicism and apathy more character-istic of our time than the framers'. For example, funda-mentalist religious groups have taken over various local school boards right under the noses of unwatchful local majorities. Perhaps intensely focused and well-organized minorities can exert disproportionate influence at the federal level too, as Madison's modern-day opponents charge, but, as this example suggests, empowering state and local gov-ernment is no solution.

So doubtful are the arguments in favor of devolution of federal power to the states that it seems likely other impuls-es might well be at work. Decentralization can be an attrac-tive cover for deregulation. As Theodore Roosevelt once said, "The effective fight against adequate control and supervision of individual, and especially corporate, wealth engaged in interstate business is chiefly done under cover; and especially under the cover of an appeal to states' rights." The decentralizers may anticipate that transferring power to the states will reduce the role of government alto-gether, leaving matters once governed at the federal level not to the states but rather to the market. Why might this be so? State governments are weaker than Congress. Most states have part-time legislatures. Few pay their legislators very much. Half have imposed term limits on state repre-sentatives, which they cannot now constitutionally do to members of Congress. The decentralizers may have a hunch that state legislatures' comparative lack of experience and expertise will lead them to produce less regulation on aver-age than would Congress on the same issues. Moreover, as Madison noted, private interest groups may seek to exert disproportionate influence at the state level. Just because factional capture has gotten easier at the federal level does not mean it has gotten any harder in the states.

Like the antifederalists of the founding era, current critics of the federal government would repose less power in the federal government and more in the states. In so doing, however, they would empower the very local forces that Madison and the framers most feared. The antifederalists lost the constitutional battle at the end of the eighteenth century. Nothing has changed in two centuries to make them right at this stage.

Chapter

2

THE ASSAULT ON GOVERNMENT

by Alan Brinkley

One of the most striking developments of the last fifteen years has been the growing power of a conservative opposition not just to particular public programs, but also to the survival of the federal government as an institution capable of playing a significant role in American life. The aborted Republican revolution of 1995, and the Contract With America that formed its basis, was the most visible evidence of this assault. But it was neither the first nor, in all likelihood, the last effort to make fundamental and crippling changes in the structure of the national state.

Attacking the federal government is an old and deep American tradition, of course—one of the most powerful in our history. It has spawned countless political movements. It has helped fuel the rise of national leaders from Thomas Jefferson and Andrew Jackson to Jimmy Carter and Ronald Reagan. Throughout much of the nineteenth century, it

largely defined the Democratic party. Throughout much of
the twentieth, it has defined the Republicans. Rarely, however, has there been an assault on the institutional and even
constitutional underpinnings of American government as
fundamental as the one facing it today. Should that assault
succeed, it would make profound changes in the character
of our national government, the legacy of which could last
for generations.

*   *   *

The crippling of the federal government is, in fact, already
far advanced. The fiscal crisis of the last fifteen years, in
which both Republicans and Democrats have been com-
plicit, has placed a financial straitjacket (deplored by some,
quietly welcomed by others) on both the president and
Congress. The Clinton administration, the first presidency in
a generation to envision important new government programs, found itself a prisoner of the deficit almost from the
beginning. The Clinton health care plan, public investment,
several early proposals for welfare reform, and other initiatives were all, at least in part, its victims. The Republican
Congress, ideologically committed to scaling back government for its own reasons, has found the deficit its greatest
ally in that effort.

But the assault on government has moved far beyond
the effects of the nation's fiscal torpor. Legislative, judicial,
and other efforts have threatened the state in even more
fundamental ways. A list of some of the changes on the
conservative agenda suggests the scope of the threat:

◆   The balanced budget amendment failed in Congress in
1995 and failed again in the spring of 1996, but it is far
from dead. If enacted, it would institutionalize what is

already an informal brake on government action by subor-
dinating all public efforts to eliminating the deficit. Deficit
reduction is a worthy national goal, to be sure, but it is not
our only one. A consistently balanced budget, moreover,
deprives the government of the flexibility it needs to deal
with economic crises and other emergencies. And it holds
virtually all government activities hostage to a rigid policy
prescription that—whatever its present value—may be
wholly inappropriate for future generations. Constitutional
amendments are dangerous tools for establishing policy pri-
orities, and a constitutionally mandated balanced budget
would dramatically weaken the government's ability to promote prosperity and growth, or to do almost anything else.
That, in fact, and not deficit reduction itself, is its principal
appeal to many of its supporters.

◆   Term limits, rejected by Congress in 1995, are also likely to emerge again in the form of a constitutional amendment. Term limits would, as proponents of the idea claim,
make it more difficult for officeholders to become deeply entrenched. But such limits would also ensure a consistently
inexperienced Congress unlikely to counter the power of
the president effectively and even more liable than today's
legislature to fall prey to the influence of special interests.

◆   Requiring supermajorities in both houses of Congress
for passage of certain legislation is another part of the
antigovernment agenda. The Senate already in effect
requires a 60 percent vote on most important bills, now
that party leaders on both sides of the aisle have made the
filibuster (for the first time in our history) a routine legislative tactic. The House proposal to require a 60 percent
majority for any tax increase would ensure the defeat of
any measure, however vital, to increase government revenues.

The balanced budget amendment supported by congressional Republicans would solidify the power of minorities to
block almost any spending measure; three-fifths of the members of both houses would have to support any override.

◆   Eliminating unfunded mandates, a process begun by
legislation passed in 1995 by Congress and signed by
President Clinton, would, if taken to the lengths many conservatives have urged, destroy the most important form of
leverage the federal government has over state and local
authorities. Washington, in fact, manages very few programs directly; almost everything it funds is administered to
some degree by other levels of government, usually according to guidelines established by Congress or the federal
agencies. Some such strictures are surely ineffective and
counterproductive. But there is a critical difference between
eliminating bad guidelines and eliminating the government's
ability to establish any guidelines at all.

◆   The Supreme Court has already edged toward a major
redefinition of the relationship between the federal government and the states and between government and the market. In overturning legislation banning guns in the vicinity of
schools two years ago, it took the first step in sixty years
toward narrowing the definition of the interstate commerce
clause, the most important basis for federal action on economic issues. The Clarence Thomas dissent in the 1995 term
limits decision, in which three of the other eight justices con-
curred, sketched a vision of the relationship between federal and state power in which the national government could
do virtually nothing unless specifically enumerated in the
Constitution (which Thomas, like other conservative justices,
reads very narrowly). The Supreme Court may be one vote
away not just from changing course on such emotionally

charged issues as abortion and affirmative action but also from fundamentally redefining the limits of federal power in a way that could undo sixty years of social and economic development.

Taken together, these initiatives and other antifederalist proposals threaten to leave the national government so enfeebled that it would have little power to manage the economy, address social problems, protect the environment, or do any of the other things most Americans have come to expect it to do. Such reforms would move the United States toward becoming a balkanized republic, with fifty semiautonomous governments. They would increase, not reduce, the number of bureaucracies with which citizens would have to deal—since those government responsibilities that remain would move out of Washington into fifty different state governments and innumerable new agencies. They would accentuate the regional, economic, religious, ethnic, and racial differences that already divide us. They would leave us impotent to confront unforeseen emergencies and unexpected problems.

Some of the practical consequences of hobbling the federal government are not difficult to imagine. Critics of Washington like to argue that the state governments, with their more imaginative leaders and their greater proximity to citizens, would do a better job of administering important programs than the federal government has done. In some cases, that would no doubt be true. Society needs vigorous and effective government at every level, and the growing competence, energy, and willingness to innovate of many state and local governments in recent years is one of the heartening developments of our time. But devolving so much power to the states is nevertheless a perilous experiment. What, in fact, has been the principal concern of state governments in recent years? It has not, for the most part, been building better social programs; it has been competing with other states to attract jobs. Republican and Democratic governors alike have staked their careers on their ability to lure employers by creating more attractive environments for businesses than other states. So far, that has meant mostly various kinds of tax credits and job training assistance. But without national standards, that competition would quickly escalate into other realms: relaxing or abandoning environmental regulations, rolling back health and safety protections for workers, restricting the power of trade unions to organize employees, reducing taxes by eliminating social services to the poor (as the 1996 welfare reform bill will now make easier). Devolution of power to the states in the way many conservatives have proposed would not mean simply greater experimentation and accountability. It would also produce a vicious, competitive battle for jobs that would drive down standards of safety, health, and public services everywhere.

*　*　*

At the heart of the present debate over government is the question of where power should lie in a democratic society. Conservatives like to claim that they are trying to return power to the people themselves, a promise that resonates with populism, one of America's oldest and most powerful political traditions. The populist view, as conservatives now present it, rests on the belief that real wisdom and decency reside in the people; that if only the politicians and the government would get out of the way, the people could be trusted to manage things fairly and honestly on their own.

This is a superficially appealing message. But it bears little relationship to the actual history of populism or to the realities of our own time. The populists of the late nineteenth century, and many of their twentieth-century heirs, were indeed skeptical of centralized power, including that of the state. But they were primarily concerned about powerful private institutions such as banks, railroads, and corporations; they recognized that for individuals and communities to retain any real power in modern society, they would need the help of an energetic government to counter the weight of these private interests. "We believe," the Populist party said in its 1892 platform, "that the powers of government—in other words, of the people—should be expanded . . . to the end that oppression, injustice and poverty shall eventually cease in the land." There are now, and there were then, many reasons to question the populists' optimistic assumption that the power of government is synonymous with the power of the people. But there is also good reason to share their view that without government, ordinary people would have very little hope of ending oppression, injustice, and poverty. The contemporary conservative message, which directs its anger at government alone, ignoring the private centers of power that limit democracy, is a radical perversion of the real populist tradition, which embraced the notion of a strong national government capable of defending individuals and communities from the great, predatory organizations that had grown up to threaten them.

Reducing the power of government is not by itself a route to empowering ordinary citizens because government is not the only—not even the principal—obstacle to individual or community autonomy. Modern society has many centers of concentrated power, of which the government is not always the most important. The large interests that shape our world are more numerous and more powerful even than those the original populists decried: corporate bureaucracies, the great institutions of the media, banks and financial institutions, trade associations and lobbying groups, and many others. None of them has much accountability to individual citizens. Because most of them are national or international in scope, state and local governments cannot by themselves effectively monitor or regulate them. Far from restoring power to individuals, disabling the federal government will do precisely the opposite. It will remove the only effective check against some of the other large organizations that dominate modern life. It will leave individuals with even less control over their own fates.

Critics of government are certainly correct that many of our political institutions are often inefficient, corrupt, and insufficiently accountable. They are correct, too, in arguing that the political process does not offer enough opportunity for participation by individuals, and that voting occasionally for candidates one has had little say in choosing is a feeble substitute for truly democratic participation. The political environment of modern America is frustrating and alienating, and it badly needs change. But giving up on government—dismantling federal institutions and relying instead on an unregulated market or on relatively weak local governments—is not the route to more democracy. It is the route to less.

Chapter

3

THE CHALLENGE TO
DELIBERATIVE DEMOCRACY

by Alan Brinkley

O f the many challenges to our political system in the last years of the twentieth century, perhaps the most disturbing is the rising popular impatience with deliberative democracy and the messy process of compromise and negotiation central to it.

Representative democracy is not always, perhaps not even often, an attractive process. In recent years, moreover, it has failed conspicuously to satisfy the yearning of much of the public for solutions to some of the nation's most serious problems. But the challenge to it raises an obvious question: What is the alternative? Two broad answers are visible in contemporary public discourse—answers that also attracted support a century ago. Both suggest something important about our present discontent. Both are inadequate to the tasks confronting us.

The first is what might best be called the populist pre-scription for American politics. It is based on the assump-tion that most of the problems of our public life are a result of the frustration of popular will—by arrogant elected offi-cials, by corrupt party leaders, by insular political organi-zations, by selfish special interests. In the 1890s, the populist critique focused in part on monopolists and robber barons, but also on politics (party bosses, corrupt legislatures, rigged elections). The 1990s have seen a similar critique of politi-cians and of the selfish private interests that seem to control them. The modern populist impulse, like earlier ones, has produced a series of efforts to allow "the people" to cir-cumvent politicians and control the public sphere more directly. They include the accelerating movement to impose term limits on elected officials and the popularity of vague proposals by Ross Perot and other antiparty politicians for a direct pipeline between public opinion and public action. At the heart of the modern populist critique is a belief that government has become an alien force in American life, working chiefly to obstruct popular will. The solution, therefore, is somehow to dispense with the inconvenient institutions of representative democracy and allow the peo-ple to govern themselves directly. This populist image first became central to modern political discourse in the rhetoric (although not often the policies) of Jimmy Carter, who cam-paigned for president in 1976 by making invidious com-parisons between a bloated, insensitive, and dishonest government and an honest, decent people who were "filled with love." And it has been sustained ever since by politi-cians of both parties representing many points on the polit-ical spectrum.

Competing with the populist critique is another evalu-ation of our political ills that, for lack of a better term, might be called the antipopulist analysis. It rests on a quite different assumption: the problem with American politics is that leaders are excessively responsive to the popular will, too easily swayed by the immediate, short-term demands of unreflective voters, insufficiently willing to resist the politically appealing in the name of the larger public interest. Far from being unrepresentative of the people, politicians have become almost morbidly sensitive to public opinion. They slavishly gauge their actions by the most recent polls, the tenor of their mail, the number of phone calls they receive from constituents on this issue or that. The result is a politics in which people have, on the whole, gotten what they demanded, and what they have demanded—low taxes and high services—has produced an epic fiscal disaster that will require several generations of sacrifice to undo. And so an effective political system, according to this analysis, requires a buffer between popular will and public action. It needs, in effect, an enlightened elite, capable of seeing the nation's long-term interests through the thicket of short-term impulses.

The antipopulist critique is less politically viable and less well articulated than its populist counterpart. But it is not insignificant. It is visible in the growing popularity of the notion (promoted, again, by Ross Perot) that people steeped in the principles of business management are much better suited than "politicians" to serve the nation well. It is visible in the continuing efforts to find some extraparliamentary device to force the federal government to balance its budget—the courts, the General Accounting Office, the Constitution, anything, it seems, but representative democracy itself. It is visible in the extraordinary, and largely unchallenged, authority of presumed experts on the Federal Reserve Board to chart the course of our economy.

These two analyses of our political problems are, of course, very different, even in many ways antithetical. But they also have characteristics in common. Both rest, in the end, on the implicit premise that there is a clearly identifiable public or community interest, and that there are simple, commonsense solutions to our national problems. The goal of public life, therefore, should be to sweep away the artificial (and presumably political) obstacles to the discovery of that public interest and the identification of those solutions. We should strive, rather, to create a government that embraces the legitimate concerns of the community and addresses them. There is a basic disagreement between these two views over where a reliable conception of the public interest can be found. Populists believe it rests in the wisdom of the people; antipopulists believe it resides somewhere else—in the disinterested knowledge of trained elites or in timeless public truths inherited from earlier eras. But both stances reflect a belief that a unitary public interest exists and that it can and should be identified. Both envision a world free of political faction and selfish interests.

There is, of course, a "public interest"—a set of basic principles that it is reasonable to expect citizens of a democracy to accept and respect. Attempting to identify such principles is a worthy effort, indeed, an effort essential to the functioning of any political system. But much of today's political discourse reflects an unrealistic conception of what the idea of public interest means. The belief that a pure "public interest" exists somewhere as a kernel of true knowledge untainted by politics or parochialism, and that it provides not just an array of basic principles but a concrete set of solutions to complex problems, is an attractive thought. But it is also a myth. We may be able to agree on a broad framework of beliefs capable of organizing our political life, but any such framework will have to make room within it for conflicting conceptions of how to translate those beliefs into practice. Because in a democracy—and particularly in a democracy as vast and diverse as our own—any practical effort to solve important public problems will always be contested. As citizens of a democracy, we are obligated to provide an arena within which that contest can occur.

The vehicle available to us is representative democracy—the chaotic, frustrating, easily corrupted, but ultimately indispensable system by which our society seeks to resolve its differences and chart its future. Our best hope for dealing with our problems is not escaping from politics—not rejecting compromise and negotiation and deliberation—but rehabilitating and relegitimizing our political system and its leaders in a way that gives all Americans a sense that they have a stake in the process and a voice in its outcomes.

Politics as practiced in America today may deserve some of the opprobrium it attracts. Until the public is convinced that the electoral process is reasonably open and reasonably fair, until voters can believe that their elected representatives are serving them and not the moneyed special interests that dominate campaign finance, until Americans see that the political system can, at least at times, rise above the savage partisanship characteristic of recent years, the unpopularity of politics will likely grow.

But a political world stripped of the institutions of representative democracy—a world without systems that simultaneously express, contain, and mediate popular will—is one that no American would welcome.

Chapter

4

ON THE DISTINCTIVENESS OF THE AMERICAN POLITICAL SYSTEM

by Nelson W. Polsby

Americans of a certain age will remember that at the first opportunity after the Allied victory in World War II, the voters, fed up, so it was said, with meat shortages and the privations of war, threw out a large number of incumbent congressmen and elected a new majority. The nation embarked upon a decade or so of jitters focused upon problems of domestic security. The Truman administration, under severe Republican pressure, launched a loyalty/security program. Senator Joseph McCarthy, with his careless charges of communism in government, flourished.

This, evidently, is the way Americans celebrate global victories. Neither the dismantling of the Soviet empire nor the meltdown of the Soviet Union itself seems to have convinced Americans of the possible virtues of their own political system.

Rather, complaints about the way the United States is governed
have never been louder or more insistent, as "malaise" has given
way to "gridlock," and gridlock to "funk" as the most fash-
ionable way to describe a system the chief feature of which is
held to be an inability to cope. If presidents and leaders of
Congress, Democrats and Republicans, talk this way, never
mind advocates of one or more third parties, must they not be
right? After all, a key test of the viability of any political system
surely must be the willingness of political elites to defend it.

On these grounds alone, the American political system
is in plenty of trouble. But a nagging doubt intrudes. One
wonders whether the bashing of the political system has
been used for narrow partisan purposes and whether, also,
it is simply ill-informed.

The American government is not easy to grasp. Most
nations are much smaller than the United States, with less
space, fewer people. The Western democracies with which
the United States is most commonly compared have one-
third (Germany) to one-fifth (United Kingdom, France) the
population of the United States, and some comparison
nations (Sweden, 9 million people; Switzerland, 7 million;
Denmark or Israel, 5 million) are even smaller. Only a few
of the world's political systems—China, India, Russia,
Indonesia, Brazil—have anywhere near the population of
the United States, and most of the larger nations—perhaps
half our size, like Nigeria, Pakistan, Bangladesh, or
Mexico—are governed by tiny groups of bureaucrats, military leaders, families, or cliques of the educated. Thus, even
when the political system embraces many people, only a
few inhabit the top in the nations as large or larger than
the United States. Most democracies of medium size have
political classes that are by U.S. standards small.

In the United States, responsibilities for public policy
are not concentrated in a few hands but are spread to

dozens of different places. Take transportation policy. Roads and their policing are devolved functions of the several states, and the fifty states parcel large chunks of authority out even further to cities, towns, and boroughs within their jurisdictions. To be sure, some transportation policy is made in Washington, for example, the rules governing Amtrak or air traffic control. But the licensing of vehicles, the control of on-street parking, the maintenance of roads and ports, the routing of buses, the building of subways—in short the vast bulk of the gigantic enterprise of American public transportation policy—can be fathomed only by traipsing around the country and looking at the disparate detailed decisions and varied decisionmakers who fix the prices of taxi medallions in New York City and plow the snow off the roads in Minnesota and provide for the coordination of rapid transit routes and schedules in the San Francisco Bay area.

Transportation is only one policy area. There are dozens more, some the responsibility exclusively of national government, some all local, some mixed. These matters are much easier to sort out, and to track, in smaller and less heterogeneous nations, and in nations with unitary constitutions. Federalism, just illustrated in the field of transportation, is embedded in the American Constitution and is one source of the spread of governmental authority, but only one source.

Consider next the separation of powers, a means of organizing government at the center of the political system where power is shared among executive, legislative, and judicial branches, all for some purposes mutually dependent, for other purposes independent of one another. Consider Congress, the world's busiest and most influential national legislature. Proposals go in the door of Congress and regularly emerge transformed by exposure to the complexities of the lawmaking process. Unlike parliamentary bodies that run on the

Westminster plan, Congress is an entity independent of the
executive branch. Its members are elected state by state, district by district, by voters to whom they are directly responsible. Members are expected to have opinions about public
policies, to respond to the concerns of their constituents, and
to participate as individuals in the making of laws.

To be sure, Congress has its division of labor; not every
member sits on every committee. And who within Congress
gets what primary responsibilities is orchestrated by partisan
caucuses and party leaders. So the fate of any particular proposal depends greatly on where it is sent—to which subcommittees and committees, superintended by which
members. Congress cannot have strong party responsibility
without sacrificing some of the advantages of this division of
labor, which allows committee specialists to acquire authority over the subject matter in their jurisdictions by learning
over time about the substance of public policy. Federalism
supports the separation of powers by giving members of
Congress roots in their own communities, where local nominating procedures for Congress lie mostly beyond the reach
of the president, and of central government.

Beside these two interacting constitutional features—
federalism and separation of powers—sits a strong judiciary,
fully empowered to review acts of political branches and to
reject those acts contradictory to the provisions of the written constitution. The strength of the judiciary evolved as a
natural consequence of the existence of enumerated, explicit rights—a Bill of Rights, in fact—that ordinary citizens pos-
sess, mostly phrased as restraints on the government. How
can an individual citizen assert these rights except through
appeal to the courts? Once courts respond to the piecemeal
invocation of the Bill of Rights by citizens, a strong and independent judiciary, and a political system dominated by
lawyers, is given a strong evolutionary preference.

Many political systems have one or more of these distinctive features of the American constitutional order: federalism, a separation of powers, a Bill of Rights. All three features, working together in the very large American arena, produce a decentralized party system with its devolved nominations and highly localized public policy preferences, a vibrant, hard to coordinate, independent legislative branch, and lawyers and lawsuits galore.

Giving up any or all of these distinctive features of the American "real-life constitution" is urged mostly in the interests of centralized authority and hierarchical coordination. Most modern democracies, it is pointed out, do without distinctively American constitutional trappings. Why cannot the United States do the same? Perhaps we could if the government of a smaller, more homogeneous nation were at stake. But when the governed are spread far and wide, and are deeply divided by race, religion, and national origin, civil peace may well require political instruments sufficiently decentralized to produce widespread acceptance of national policies and tolerance of national politicians. Although the American system is weak in forward motion, it is strong in its capacity to solicit the marks of legitimacy: acceptance of decisions, willingness to go along, loyalty in time of emergency.

It is, according to this interpretation of the emergent design of the Constitution, thus no accident that the one major period of constitutional breakdown into civil war could be understood as a matter of a failure of center-periphery accommodation. Civil War-era theories of nullification, states' rights, and concurrent majorities were all attempts to fashion an even more devolved constitution, one that could contain the enormity of slavery. As this episode teaches, and as observers of events in the modern world from Beirut to Bosnia might attest, obtaining the

consent of the governed when the body politic is heterogeneous is no mean feat.

American democracy, on this reading, is more democratic than any of the large, complex nations in the world,
and larger and more complex than all of the other democratic nations (save India). Proposals for change that appre-
ciate the size and complexity of the system have a better
chance of success than proposals that merely complain that
the system is sizable and complicated. Judging from the success of smaller democratic nations, Madison was clearly
wrong in arguing that a large, extended republic was necessary to prevent tyranny. But he was undoubtedly right in
observing that an extended republic is what the United States
would become. In 1787, soon after the Constitution was
written, it is recorded that "a lady asked Benjamin Franklin,
'Well, Doctor, what have we got, a republic or a monarchy.'
'A republic,' replied the Doctor, 'if you can keep it.'"

Part
2

*Modern Politics and
Its Discontents*

Chapter

5

THE AMERICAN PARTY SYSTEM

by Nelson W. Polsby

The purpose of a political party is to organize activities that put people in public office—especially elective office. A party *system* is the organization that governs the relations between parties and elections, and in complex democratic societies it largely determines the means by which citizens and their concerns are represented by political parties.

The American party system, like so many features of the American political landscape, is singular in its design. Because so much in the way of politics—including elections—takes place at state and local levels in the American federal system, party activity is concentrated at those levels and is principally regulated by the states. Parties exist at the national level as well since they also operate to nominate presidents, to collect and disburse soft money, to recruit candidates for some congressional seats, and to coordinate the organization of Congress.

One of the singularities of the American party system is that, despite the size and the heterogeneity of the nation, the United States makes do with only two major parties, Democratic and Republican. An overwhelming number of American public officials are elected under one label or the other, and most ordinary citizens "identify" either as Democrats or Republicans.

Why only two parties? The way American elections are structured encourages a duopoly: one party in power, the other out. Officials are elected from single-member districts and win office by coming out ahead of competitors, in a system for determining winners called "first-past-the-post." First-past-the-post encourages voters favoring candidates who are out of office to club together in a single "out" party. This incentive structure cuts down on the number of plausible challengers to incumbents but increases the strength of the challenge, thus creating a situation that is thought to increase the solicitude of incumbents toward the needs and demands of ordinary citizens.

It is, to most thoughtful observers, intuitively obvious that a two-party system of government better serves the interests of democracy than a one-party system. Two parties, in the constitutional presence of reasonably frequent elections, means that a possibility exists that those citizens disagreeing with the government or its policies have the lively option of aggregating themselves behind the banner of a party capable of replacing the government. The mere existence of this option, it is believed, changes the attitudes and behavior of incumbents, who as a result take an interest in a greater variety of public opinions. These conditions presumably mean less arbitrariness in government.

What is not so obvious is the superiority of a two-party system over a system of three or more parties. For the following argument I am greatly in the debt of students of the subdiscipline of social choice, notably the economist Kenneth Arrow, who elegantly proved that a choice process following simple democratic rules could readily produce unsatisfactory outcomes when three or more options were available.

At first blush, the idea of there being more than one antigovernmental option might suggest a more nuanced opportunity to express accurately a broader range of the political sentiments that may exist in a population—especially a large population. Thus the intuitive appeal of a three-or-more-party system to democratic sensibilities. But there are problems: consider what spreading the anti-incumbent vote among several options does for electoral outcomes in a first-past-the-post regime. This arrangement, by dividing the opposition, helps the status quo. Presumably, the knowledge that the opposition is divided reduces incumbents' perceived vulnerability, which may induce in them complacency, arbitrariness, and indifference to popular sentiment.

Consider also the difficulty of arriving at any result at all if preferences are spread among three well-organized options, A, B, and C. Suppose some voters prefer the options in the order given: A-B-C. Others prefer B-C-A. And others prefer C-A-B. When preferences are arrayed in this fashion, no result is possible that gratifies a majority. Means other than simple obedience to majority rule must be found for resolving this famous paradox of social choice. Such considerations have led thoughtful people to the conclusion that it is not such a bad idea to organize incentives so that elections, rather than these other, unspecified means, bear the burden of channeling popular preferences into two, rather than more than two, streams.

Realistically, however, where the underlying population is large and heterogeneous, it is improbable that as few as two points of view will actually exist. Two mechanisms currently exist for dealing with this dilemma. One is proportional representation, a family of procedures in which voters get to rank their preferences, or are given two or more ballots to cast, or have their votes counted so as to produce winners even though less than a majority or only a plurality voted for them. The American solution is the other: territorial division.

In America the same political labels—Democratic and Republican—cover virtually all public officeholders, and therefore most voters are everywhere mobilized in the name of these two parties. Yet Democrats and Republicans are not everywhere the same. Variations—sometimes subtle, sometimes blatant—in the fifty political cultures of the states yield considerable differences overall in what it means to be, or to vote, Democratic or Republican. These differences suggest that one may be justified in referring to the American two-party system as masking something more like a hundred-party system.

To be sure, at any particular place on the map the political options may look too sparse for many local voters. Electoral arrangements requiring only a plurality of votes to win offices on local ballots—the first-past-the-post system—strongly encourage limitations in the number of well-organized alternatives. The challenge to sectional, regional, and local parties is to aim their appeals at sectional, regional, and local sentiments. If they did not there would be considerable pressure toward adopting one (or more) of the proportional representation mechanisms for counting votes and allocating legislative seats. But since the Georgia Republican party endeavors to appeal to Georgia Republican voters without making any attempt to coordinate with Republican party leaders in Vermont or Wisconsin (and the same, mutatis mutandis, for Democrats), most voters find local options sufficiently to their liking so that there is little or no popular interest in systemic change.

Occasionally third parties come along and for a while capture important segments of the market for votes. Typically, at the national level they have very little staying power over the long run since one or both major parties customarily steal their issues. Local or sectional third parties like New York City's Liberal party or the late Farmer-Labor party of Minnesota last longer in special circumstances, but usually because they are the direct expression of well-organized local interest groups more or less in electoral collusion with one of the major parties.

Arguably, a two-party setup is suspect because even with a large number of local and regional variations it cannot begin to capture and therefore represent the rich stew of opinions that may exist in an enormous and diverse population. In the United States, two further factors mitigate this nagging problem. The first is the stark acknowledgment that under any system that pretends to practicality, ultimately, decisions must be reached and not everyone can get his or her way. Parties are as much engaged in prioritizing choices, and therefore suppressing some of them, as they are in expressing alternatives that may exist in the minds of ordinary citizens. Thus, one significant test of a party system is the extent to which it enjoys legitimacy as parties go about the task of prioritizing, that is, the extent to which they are regarded as an acceptable vehicle for gratifying some interest groups and not others. On the whole, this prioritizing activity is commonly seen (with good reason) as a strength of American parties. Many interests, though to be sure not all, get into the game under a system of sharply localized elections held frequently, even though successful candidates are required only to be the first past the post.

The second condition countervailing the representational limitations of the American two-party system is the fact that, on many issues of public policy, public opinion is

unformed and very largely responsive to signals from political leaders. This means the presumption that the systemic
limitation of only two parties inhibits the expression of a
panoply of nuanced alternatives residing in the hearts and
minds of the populace at large is, over a wide range of significant issues, almost certainly empirically false: no such
attitudes exist. Attitudes on many, perhaps most, public
issues are stimulated and evoked by the politicians who
must consider them; for these purposes, two parties are normally sufficient to inspire alertness in political leaders to
the interests of their constituents.

It must be said also that none of the alternatives to a
two-party system are without practical difficulties. It is not
much of a criticism to point out that a given set of decisionmaking processes (like first-past-the-post) denies some
people the outcomes they want. All decisionmaking processes, operating in the absence of unanimity, do that. And
indeed, the requirement of unanimity is arguably the least
democratic process of all since tiny minorities can in such
circumstances thwart the will of many.

Better questions to ask are whether a decisionmaking
process lets in sufficient fresh air to provide for real political competition: whether debate about public policies is
robust, whether incumbents in office behave as though they
are obliged to listen. By these criteria the hundred-party
system that Americans operate under two labels seems at
least as successful as most imaginable alternatives, and it
seems to work quite well in practice.

Because it is commonly believed that dissatisfaction
with alternatives on offer causes widespread abstention
from voting in the United States, it should be said that there
is little or no respectable evidence sustaining this notion.
Citizens expressing varying degrees of dissatisfaction with
electoral politics vote with just about the same frequency as

citizens happier with "the system." And so there are no grounds for imagining that if Americans could choose from a broader menu of parties in each locality more of them would vote. In fact, under the laws of many states, minor parties—sometimes a great many minor parties—already make available alternative candidates for many public offices. But very few Americans vote for them.

Chapter

6

THE PRESIDENTIAL CAMPAIGN, BRITISH STYLE

by Nelson W. Polsby

Every four years the United States launches a presidential
election marathon, and every four years intelligent Americans
complain about the wasted time, the distraction, the spent
energy, and the costs of it all. We hear, once more, the peren-
nial questions, the most famous of which is "Why can't we do
things with less fuss, the way they do it in England?" Let us
see if we can give better answers this time around.

Q. In England, when they have a national election, the
whole thing takes only three weeks. Why can't we do it
the way they do it in England?

A. We can!

Q. How? What would it take?

A. Easy. First, abolish the presidency.

Q. What do you mean?

A. There is no British president. They haven't got one. That's why they have no presidential election.

Q. But who runs the country?

A. Bureaucrats, mostly. They are very powerful, much more so than in the United States. And the prime minister and cabinet, called "the government."

Q. Who are they?

A. Elected members of Parliament, plus one or two lords, who are picked out of the House of Lords by the prime minister.

Q. Who is . . .

A. The elected head of the party having the most members in Parliament.

Q. OK, what about these elections?

A. Here are the rules. Political parties put up candidates in each parliamentary constituency—there are 651 of them—where they think they have a chance. Whichever candidate gets the most votes wins and goes to Parliament. Each party in Parliament has different rules for picking its leader. The leader of the party with the most members is asked by the queen to form a government, that is, pick a cabinet. The cabinet makes policy and, together with the departments of government, staffed by career bureaucrats, governs the country.

Q. Parliament sounds like Congress.

A. It is, a little. Except elections to Congress take place every two years, at a fixed time. Parliamentary elections have to occur within a five-year period but may be held whenever the prime minister decides.

Q. Therefore?

A. Therefore, the parties in each constituency must be ready to conduct the election at any time. Therefore, there is no consolidated nomination process like the American presidential primaries that drives everybody crazy. Therefore, even as we speak, in most constituencies there are party nominees ready to go. These candidates campaign in small ways all the time, whether there is an election pending or not. It's called "nursing the constituency."

Q. How do people get to be party nominees?

A. The two major parties do it slightly differently. In the Labour party, candidates are elected at a meeting of constituency party members from short lists drawn up by a local committee of party leaders. The nomination must then be approved by national party leaders. Conservatives choose their candidate from a national list whose membership is controlled by party national headquarters. Candidates can be from anywhere; members of Parliament are usually not from the places they represent in Parliament.

Q. So how can they represent local interests?

A. Some members move into their constituencies and do their best to listen to the locals. But of course they can't do much for them; it's party leaders in Parliament and bureaucrats that run the government. Ordinary members of Parliament are there to vote to support their party leaders. If ordinary members of the governing party don't go along with party policy when they vote, they may bring a new election down on their heads, which they might lose. Members have very little in the way of staff or access to information. And, after all, they were screened by national party headquarters in the first place.

Q. But the campaigns are short, right?

A. Right. About three weeks. Each party gets free television time on the national networks, roughly proportional to their success at the polls the previous time. Local campaigns consist mostly of speechmaking at meetings. Constituencies are small in population, about a tenth the size of congressional districts. Expenditures for advertising are restricted, but of course with small constituencies, nominees already picked and usually therefore reasonably well known, and voting that strongly reflects party allegiances since individual members cannot do much anyway, there isn't much need for campaign money at the level of the individual constituency. Anyway, it's illegal.

Q. They don't need it?

A. No, they don't. The national parties saturate the airwaves for about a month with their party promises and manifestos and leaders. These are what the country is going to get if they are elected, and so that is what voters need to know about.

Q. OK. So we abolish the presidency and we elect only members of Congress. Now, how do I get to pick the leaders of Congress?

A. You don't.

Q. You mean?

A. You go to the polls and make one X. That X helps elect a member of Congress from your district—if you are on the winning side. The members have picked their leader. The leader runs the country. You don't get involved in a complicated leadership nominating process. Money is saved. Time is saved. Energy is saved. It is not confusing.

Q. But wouldn't that mean less representation for ordinary citizens? Less access to government? More centralized decisionmaking? Less legitimacy for public policy?

A. If you don't want it, don't ask for it.

Chapter

7

MONEY IN PRESIDENTIAL CAMPAIGNS

by Nelson W. Polsby

Many thoughtful Americans are worried about the influence of money in presidential campaigns, but virtually all proposed solutions entail serious difficulties. This means that the problem deserves more discussion.

What, in the first place, is the problem? Here is one interpretation:

It is unseemly and unfair that extremely rich individuals, spending enormous amounts of their own money, can run for high public office completely unconstrained by the sorts of regulations on how much can be accepted or spent that bind candidates who are spending other people's money and accepting federal subsidies. This advantage to candidates spending their own money is the result of a Supreme Court decision holding that the power to advertise our own opinions and preferences is protected by the First Amendment to the Constitution but that acceptance of a public subsidy can be regulated.

Possible solutions to this problem point in at least two directions. In one direction would be a constitutional amendment depriving rich candidates of a First Amendment right they now enjoy and confining unbridled First Amendment protection only to those individuals who control access to the news media. This might mean that an expenditure limitation could prevent a candidate from taking out an advertisement in a newspaper to rebut attacks on that newspaper's front page.

Considerations of this sort point to an alternative solution. Instead of tightening regulations on the rich, what about relaxing regulations on other candidates, making it possible for them to raise and spend money more freely? This might mean more cash in the system raised from private sources, or direct or in-kind public subsidies, such as vouchers permitting free or cut-rate access to television time.

Reformers have to decide whether what they are after is a system in which all candidates have access to equal resources—which implies ceilings on expenditures applicable equally to all—or a system in which all reasonable candidates have access to enough resources to make their case. This latter system implies that subsidies should act more as floors than ceilings, and it takes account of the fact that equal resources do not level the field if one of the players is an incumbent or is on other grounds already famous.

The reason large amounts of money are needed by candidates in the American political system is because the nation is large—the third most populous in the world—and nomination processes are relatively open and uncontrolled by strong political parties. Large numbers of individual voters must therefore be reached by candidates. A lot of money is spent for television advertising and for achieving name recognition, problems that do not exist in nations where electorates are small or candidates can rely on strong political parties for nomination and campaign help. Thus, while the sheer amount of money used by various campaigners is often seen as the problem, it could be argued that this is the price we pay for a system with weak party leadership that makes it essential for many candidates to campaign—thus driving up total expenditures—and that the need to appeal to large numbers of voters in primary elections must be taken into account.

Another way of looking at the problem of money in elections is to look not at expenditures but at contributions. Do not contributions establish unwholesome relations between contributors and the candidates amounting, in extreme cases, to the equivalent of bribery? Rich individuals spending their own money can claim that since they have no contributors, they have no obligations.

There is a limit to the desirability of this arrangement. Leaders ought not to be totally detached from alliances with followers in a healthy democratic system, since democracy normally requires that followers and their concerns play a large part in forming the agendas and preferences of leaders. Leaders and followers can come into agreement by virtue of shared ideology or concordance of views, and followers may without criminal intent wish to support leaders with whom they agree. There is no foolproof way of distinguishing these blameless conditions from bribery (in which interest groups take the initiative) or extortion (in which politicians take the initiative).

Legal limitations on the amounts of money that can pass between individuals running for office and donors constitute an attempt to steer clear of these difficulties, but loopholes abound. Donors can express support—and possibly gain influence—by steering the contributions of others, by bundling contributions from diverse sources, or by contributing indirectly to ancillary organizations like parties or interest groups operating independently of candidate organizations. A grim pursuit seeking to close down each and every one of these loopholes soon trenches on the First Amendment rights of citizens to give publicity or effect to their political opinions.

Thus, efforts to limit both expenditures and contributions run up against more fundamental systemic constraints: a large electorate, weak parties, and a Constitution that protects political expression broadly construed. On the whole, the most promising line of attack, given these constraints, may be one that puts some trust in the idea that the law of diminishing returns sooner or later will mitigate the effects of large expenditures and that relies upon strong disclosure requirements to help competitors and the voting public monitor the sources of funds that signal the alliances candidates are making.

There remains the issue of ensuring adequate competitiveness. This requires not that less well funded candidates in their profusion have amounts of money equal to the richest candidates in the field, but that decent numbers of them have enough to make their case to the mass media and to at least enough voters in primary elections to permit lightning to strike, if it is destined to do so. This, presumably, would constitute a rationale in defense of some sort of public subsidy. But what sort? Obviously, some limitations on the largesse of taxpayers have to exist. At the moment, matching-fund formulas are in place that tend to favor candidates with the best and most expensive fund-raising organizations.

More effective in putting less well heeled candidates on a stronger footing have been the debates and public forums that are staged in early primary states and frequently broadcast nationwide. These public service events are taking up some important slack in a system that has not solved the complicated, indeed probably unsolvable, problem of electoral finance.

Chapter

8

CAMPAIGN FINANCE REFORM: A RESPONSE TO NELSON W. POLSBY

by Alan Brinkley

Nelson Polsby's provocative essay makes clear that the present system of campaign finance is not simply the result of a corrupt conspiracy among politicians and special interests, as many Americans seem to believe. It is, above all, the result of the great difficulty many candidates face in trying to reach a large and far-flung electorate—and the enormous expenses many of them occur in attempting to do so. Running for office in America costs a great deal of money, and it is unrealistic to expect candidates not to try to find the funds they need in whatever ways are legally open to them.

Polsby also points out what a generation of efforts to reform campaign finance has already made clear: that it is extremely difficult to design a system that is capable of raising enough money to support viable campaigns and that is, at the same time, impervious to abuse. Virtually every

change in campaign finance law over the past thirty years
has made the system worse rather than better. It may be
naive to assume that another round of reforms will be any
more successful.

But the arguments for tolerating the present system of
campaign finance must be weighed against the costs that system imposes on our politics. And the cost has become intol-
erably high. As things now stand, the process of financing
campaigns is a source of extraordinary impropriety and corruption in the conduct of public affairs. Perhaps equally
important, it is among the most important factors eroding
popular trust in government and the political process. To concede that it is the best we can do is to concede that our public
world is not capable of functioning honorably or credibly.

That the present system feeds the corruption of public
life is almost impossible to challenge. In the 104th Congress,
some Republican leaders made no secret of their willingness
to promote legislation favorable to particular groups because
they had promised those groups they would do so in exchange for campaign contributions, and industry lobbyists—
having contributed heavily to the campaigns of congressional
leaders—worked openly with committee staffs in drafting
legislation that would affect them. But what made those
events significant was only that the legislators in question
made so little effort to hide them. Few members of Congress
of either party could honestly argue that there is no connection between the campaign contributions they receive
and the positions they take; as the costs of campaigns rise
and the fund-raising activities of elected officials become
an almost constant fact of life, those connections become
ever more difficult to avoid.

That the present system erodes popular trust in the
process is even more difficult to refute. Public opinion polls
consistently reveal that voters have experienced a massive

loss of faith in their public officials. They reveal too that many of those who have lost faith have done so in large part because they believe politics is run by money for the benefit of the wealthy and special interests. Cynicism about politics and government is so widespread, and so readily confirmed by the behavior of the system, that it is almost impossible to imagine a restoration of popular faith without a significant demonstration by the political community that it understands and means to respond to the sources of the public's contempt.

It is much easier to state the problems with the present system of campaign finance than it is to envision a desirable alternative to it. And it is also much easier to suggest reforms than to imagine a political scenario likely to result in their adoption. The people who will vote on any reforms are, of course, the same people who benefit most from the present system. And the likelihood of most significant reforms withstanding the scrutiny of the Supreme Court is in serious doubt in light of the 1976 *Buckley* v. *Valeo* decision, in which the Court declared limits on political spending by individuals a violation of free speech. The present Court seems more likely to limit even further Congress's ability to restrict spending than to reverse its position of twenty years ago.

Even so, there are ways to reform campaign finance that might survive judicial scrutiny and that could make some difference. Some critics of the present system have argued that what our politics needs is more, not less, money. But recent campaigns suggest exactly the opposite. The enormous campaign budgets of recent years have made election seasons a source of widespread dismay. They have permitted many candidates to wage virtual war with one another over the airwaves with commercials that are often savage and seldom informative; and they have encouraged them to avoid face-to-face contact with voters or with each other. Big money seems to degrade politics, not—as some argue—to open it up.

One route to an improved political world, therefore, lies in closing the enormous loopholes in the present laws that permit virtually unlimited contributions to party organizations and other groups ostensibly unconnected to particular campaigns (what has come to be known as "soft money"). If candidates could be made to fund their campaigns solely on the basis of money they raise from individuals (whose contributions are presently restricted to $1,000), the savage competition for dollars might de-escalate, and the campaigns themselves might regain at least a degree of civility and substance.

Among other possible reforms are public support for campaigns for federal office in exchange for acceptance of spending limits; the provision of free television time to candidates if they forgo advertising beyond a certain level; limiting out-of-state or out-of-district contributions to candidates for Congress; a more effective and timely process of disclosure; and—a favorite of many advocates of change even if exceedingly unlikely to succeed—persuading the Court to overturn *Buckley* v. *Valeo.*

No plausible reform will solve all the problems of campaign finance. Some might end up, as previous reforms have done, making things worse. But the difficulties are no excuse for inaction. Those who are disgusted by the sight of a political arena so consumed by fund-raising and so awash in money that ethical boundaries are almost impossible to sustain—a group that includes, if recent experience is any indication, most Americans—should insist that we continue to look for a system capable both of sustaining the electoral process and giving it at least a shred of moral legitimacy.

Part 3

The Constitution in a Word Processor

Chapter
9

WHAT'S WRONG WITH CONSTITUTIONAL AMENDMENTS?

by Kathleen M. Sullivan

Most things Congress does can be undone by the next election. Amendments to the U.S. Constitution cannot. And yet recent Congresses have been stricken with constitutional amendment fever. More constitutional amendment proposals have been taken seriously now than at any other recent time. Some have even come close to passing. An amendment calling for a balanced budget passed the House twice and came within one and then two votes of passing in the Senate. An amendment allowing punishment of flag burners easily passed the House and fell just three votes short in the Senate. These and other proposed amendments continue to circulate— including amendments that would impose term limits on members of Congress, permit subsidies for religious speech with public funds, confer procedural rights upon crime victims, denaturalize children of illegal immigrants, or require a three-fifths vote to raise taxes, to name a few.

Many of these amendments are bad ideas. But they are dangerous apart from their individual merits. The Constitution was, as Chief Justice John Marshall once wrote, "intended to endure for ages to come." Thus, it should be amended sparingly, not used as a chip in short-run political games. This was clearly the view of the framers, who made the Constitution extraordinarily difficult to amend. Amendments can pass only by the action of large supermajorities. Congress may propose amendments by a two-thirds vote of both houses. Or the legislatures of two-thirds of the states may request that Congress call a constitutional convention. Either way, a proposed amendment becomes law only when ratified by three-fourths of the states. Once an amendment clears these hurdles into the Constitution, it is equally difficult to remove.

Not surprisingly, the Constitution has been amended only twenty-seven times in our history. Half of these arose in exceptional circumstances. Ten made up the Bill of Rights, added in one fell swoop by the First Congress and ratified in 1791 as part of a bargain that induced reluctant states to accept the Constitution. And the Thirteenth, Fourteenth, and Fifteenth amendments, which abolished slavery and gave African-Americans rights of equal citizenship, were passed by the Reconstruction Congress in the wake of the Civil War.

The remaining amendments have tinkered little with the original constitutional design. Four extended the right to vote in federal elections to broader classes of citizens: the Fifteenth to racial minorities, the Nineteenth to women, the Twenty-fourth to voters too poor to pay a poll tax, and the Twenty-sixth to persons between the ages of eighteen and twenty-one. Only two amendments ever tried to impose a particular social policy: the Eighteenth Amendment imposed

Prohibition and the Twenty-first repealed it. Only two amendments changed the original structure of the government: the Seventeenth Amendment provided for popular election of senators, and the Twenty-second imposed a two-term limit on the presidency. And only four amendments have ever been enacted to overrule decisions of the Supreme Court. The remaining handful of amendments were national housekeeping measures, the most important of which was the Twenty-fifth Amendment's establishment of procedures for presidential succession. We have never had a constitutional convention.

Our traditional reluctance to amend the Constitution stands on good reason today, the will of the framers aside. This is not because the Constitution deserves idolatry— Thomas Jefferson cautioned in 1816 that we should not treat it "like the ark of the covenant, too sacred to be touched." It is rather because maintaining stable agreement on the fundamental organizing principles of government has a number of clear political advantages over a system whose basic structure is always up for grabs. As James Madison cautioned in *The Federalist* No. 43, we ought to guard "against that extreme facility" of constitutional amendment "which would render the Constitution too mutable." What are the reasons this might be so?

First, it is a bad idea to politicize the Constitution. The very idea of a constitution turns on the separation of the legal and the political realms. The Constitution sets up the framework of government. It also sets forth a few fundamental political ideals (equality, representation, individual liberties) that place limits on how far any temporary majority may go. This is our higher law. All the rest is left to politics. Losers in the short run yield to the winners out of respect for the constitutional framework set up for the long run. This makes the peaceful conduct of ordinary

politics possible. Without such respect for the constitutional framework, politics would degenerate into fractious
war. But the more a constitution is politicized, the less it
operates as a fundamental charter of government. The
more a constitution is amended, the more it seems like ordinary legislation.

Two examples are instructive. The only modern federal
constitutional amendment to impose a controversial social
policy was a failure. The Eighteenth Amendment introduced
Prohibition, and, fourteen years later, the Twenty-first
Amendment repealed it. As Justice Oliver Wendell Holmes,
Jr., once wrote, "a constitution is not meant to embody a
particular economic theory," for it is "made for people of
fundamentally differing views." Amendments that embody
a specific and debatable social or economic policy allow
one generation to tie the hands of another, entrenching
approaches that ought to be revisable in the crucible of ordinary politics. Thus it is not surprising that the only amendment to the U.S. Constitution ever to impose such a policy
is also the only one ever to be repealed.

Now consider the experience of the states. In contrast to
the spare federal Constitution, state constitutions are typically voluminous tomes. Most state constitutions are amend-
able by simple majority, including by popular initiative and
referendum. While the federal Constitution has been amended only twenty-seven times in more than two hundred years,
the fifty state constitutions have suffered a total of nearly
six thousand amendments. They have thus taken on what
Marshall called in *McCulloch* v. *Maryland* "the prolixity of
a legal code"—a vice he praised the federal Constitution for
avoiding. State constitutions are loaded with particular provisions resembling ordinary legislation and embodying the
outcome of special interest deals. As a result, they command
far less respect than the U.S. Constitution.

A second reason to resist writing short-term policy goals into the Constitution is that they nearly always turn out to have bad and unintended structural consequences. This is in part because amendments are passed piecemeal. In contrast, the Constitution was drafted as a whole at Philadelphia. The framers had to think about how the entire thing fit together. Not so for modern amendments. Consider congressional term limits, for example. Term limits amendment advocates claim that rotating incumbents out of office would decrease institutional responsiveness to special interests and make the federal legislation more responsive to popular will. But would it? There's a better chance that term limits would shift power from Congress to the permanent civil service that staffs the executive branch and agencies, where special interest influence would remain untouched.

To take another example, advocates of the balanced budget amendment focus on claims that elimination of the deficit will help investment and growth. But they ignore the structural consequences of shifting fiscal power from Congress to the president or the courts. The power of the purse was intentionally entrusted by the framers to the most representative branch. As Madison wrote in *The Federalist* No. 58, the taxing and spending power is "the most complete and effectual weapon with which any constitution can arm the immediate representatives of the people." The balanced budget amendment, however, would tempt the president to impound funds, or at least threaten to do so in order to gain greater leverage over Congress. And it would tempt the courts to enter a judicial quagmire for which they are ill-equipped. When is the budget in balance? Whose estimates should we use? What if growth turns out faster than expected? Lawsuits over these questions could drag on for years. Such redistribution of power among the federal branches surely should not be undertaken lightly, especially not under the pressure of an election year.

A third danger lurking in constitutional amendments is that of mutiny against the authority of the Supreme Court. We have lasted two centuries with only twenty-seven amendments because the Supreme Court has been given enough interpretive latitude to adapt the basic charter to changing times. Our high court enjoys a respect and legitimacy uncommon elsewhere in the world. That legitimacy is salutary, for it enables the Court to settle or at least defuse society's most ideologically charged disputes.

Contemporary constitutional revisionists, however, suggest that if you dislike a Supreme Court decision, mobilize to overturn it. If the Court holds that free speech rights protect flag burners, just write a flag-burning exception into the First Amendment. If the Court limits student prayer in public schools, rewrite the establishment clause to replace neutrality toward religion with equal rights for religious access instead. Such amendment proposals no doubt reflect the revisionists' frustration that court packing turns out to be harder than it seems—Presidents Reagan and Bush, as it turned out, appointed more moderate than conservative justices. But undermining the authority of the institution itself is an unwise response to such disappointments.

In any event, it is illusory to think that an amendment will somehow eliminate judicial discretion. Most constitutional amendment proposals are, like the original document, written in general and open-ended terms. Thus, they necessarily defer hard questions to ultimate resolution by the courts. Does the balanced budget amendment give the president impoundment power? Congress settled this matter by statute with President Nixon, but the amendment would reopen the question. Does splattering mustard on your Fourth of July flag napkin amount to flag desecration? A committee of senators got nowhere trying to write language that would guarantee against such an absurd result. Would unisex bathrooms have been mandated if the Equal Rights Amendment had ever passed? Advocates on both sides debated the issue fiercely, but only the Supreme Court would ever have decided for sure.

For the most part we have managed to keep short-term politics out of the rewriting of the fundamental charter. Now is no time to start. Of course, on rare occasions, constitutional amendments are desirable. We have passed various structural amendments to tie our hands against short-term sentiments, for example, through the amendments expanding the right to vote. But unless the ordinary give-and-take of our politics proves incapable of solving something, the Constitution is not the place to go to fix it.

Chapter

10

TERM LIMITS

by Nelson W. Polsby

T he Supreme Court has ruled that efforts in several
states to limit the terms of members of Congress are unconstitutional. This ruling supplements an earlier decision for-
bidding Congress from adding to the qualifications for its
own members set down explicitly in the Constitution, namely age—twenty-five for House members, thirty for senators—
American citizenship, and residence within the state where
the candidate is running at the time of election. So, presumably, advocates of term limits will now seek a constitutional amendment to accomplish what appears still to be
the overwhelmingly popular goal of putting a cap on the
time that any individual can serve in the U.S. Congress.

Advocates differ in the stringency of their preferred
limitation—six years or twelve years, lifetime ban or limit
on consecutive service, immediate or prospective application. These details have stimulated disagreements, even

unexpectedly ferocious little battles, among advocates—
mainly, one supposes, because advocates perceive themselves to have won the main battle, with public opinion so
much in favor of the general idea.

But because term limits are such a very bad idea, the
merits of the policy deserve more thorough consideration as
the battleground shifts to the constitutional amendment
process. The main effect of this measure is overwhelmingly
likely to be the weakening of Congress in the overall scheme
of national policymaking. Weakening Congress means
reducing the influence of public deliberation by elected representatives of the American people in the making of public
policy. It means a migration of power away from those public officials—members of Congress—most accessible to ordinary citizens and into the hands of unelected bureaucrats
and congressional staff, the admittedly elected but far more
distant president and his largely unaccountable entourage of
appointed officials, and, most unacceptably, lobbyists and
interest group specialists in public policy. Most of these participants are highly legitimate and frequently constitutionally protected—in the case of lobbyists, through the right of
petition. But we do not elect them. The people are entitled
to a Congress capable of maintaining an arm's-length independence from them, and term limits will deny Congress
that capability.

How is this reduction in congressional power likely to
take place? Mainly through the operation of two well-
known, easily anticipated, and complementary mechanisms:
loss of substantive experience by the membership in aggregate and the corresponding exponential growth of direct
dependence by members upon interest groups.

1. EXPERIENCE: Experience at the rather complicated work of
Congress really does increase the effectiveness of individual

members and improves the collective legislative product. One would think that this would appeal to common sense. In virtually all sorts of work, experience enhances effectiveness. The issues that regularly come before Congress are not all straightforward. Some require technical mastery. Others demand understanding of political crosscurrents of various sorts. Many require deliberation, the consideration of claims and counterclaims in a setting in which members do not work alone but in groups: committees, subcommittees, task forces, caucuses of varying sizes and shapes. Conscientious members—and there are many—are not merely striving to decide whether to vote up or down on the final passage of bills but also seeking to understand, and sometimes to contribute to, the substance of measures that the entire body must consider. There are alternative possibilities that need to be explored, amendments to be weighed, and bargains to be struck as Congress moves toward the enactment of public policy.

This is all serious work. It is perfectly true that members of Congress, being ultimately responsible only to the electorates in their home districts, have great leeway in the extent to which they apply themselves to legislative tasks. Some specialize narrowly. Some seek publicity rather than the rewards of substantive mastery. Some are lazy and some untalented. But many work at legislating. As a body, Congress accepts more substantive responsibility entailing the independent weighing of alternatives than any legislature on the face of the earth. Despite the inevitable unevenness in the abilities of members, Congress organizes to do business, mobilizes its energies, and produces work deserving of respect. Moreover, it does so while accepting the meaningful constraint that its members must as individuals stand regularly for elections in which they submit themselves to the judgment of constituents who in general have no idea what the job actually involves or how well their member does it.

Members cheerfully accept this constraint and work as best they can to convince their constituents to return them to office, with, on the whole, notable success. Members are generally popular with their constituents. But Congress as a body is not, and it is Congress as a body that will be harmed by term limits. Individual members can for the most part take care of themselves. What the American people will lose, though, by arbitrarily amputating along with the time-servers members who have learned how to legislate effectively, is access to an institution that as a collective enterprise exercises strong and sometimes detailed influence on policy-making.

2. *INTERESTS:* Arranging to banish its knowledgeable, skilled, and experienced members on a regular basis can scarcely be good for any institution with serious work to do. And this is especially true in view of the fact that, willy-nilly, the work must be done. But with term limits it will be done by less well informed and seasoned legislators, who, deprived of the option of a legislative career, are bound to be less willing to invest personally in the mastery of policy.

Such legislators would also be unusually susceptible to the influence of interested parties, most commonly taking the form of organized interest groups. This inordinate influence would occur at a minimum at three stages of the term-limited legislator's career.

In most parts of the United States, in order to enter Congress a prospective member must put together sufficient resources to run, which usually requires at least some alliances with like-minded interest groups in the constituency. Once a member is in office for a while, the interest groups usually need the member more than the member needs any particular interest group. Term limits guarantee a steady flow of new members, hence creating more situations in which the initial dependency of members on interest groups holds sway.

Even greater dependency would occur toward the end of a member's service. Term-limited members must then worry about what comes next. For many departing members, cordial relations with interest groups can provide leads into life after Congress. Able members may distinguish themselves in the evenhanded performance of their work and thus commend themselves to future employers who do regular business with Congress. Similar opportunities will also unavoidably exist for the less scrupulous.

Thus, both at the beginning and the end of a congressional career the member is unusually susceptible to interest group influence. To shrink the distance between these two points creates a bonanza for outside interests organized to take advantage of it. Inexperience at legislative work for members new to the job provides yet a third toehold for interest groups, who can supply knowledge about issues and make up for the ignorance of the newly arrived. The idea that advocates sometimes express that term limits emancipate Congress from interest groups is dubious; indeed, more likely exactly the opposite is the case.

It is evident that a dependent, relatively ignorant, inexperienced, and weak Congress is not a good thing. Ordinary Americans need the access to their government that a strong Congress can provide. For the sake of the American people, the branch that represents them and listens to them best needs to be preserved and strengthened, not crippled by term limits.

Chapter

11

DEMOCRACY AND THE
FEDERAL BUDGET

by Kathleen M. Sullivan

Among the many constitutional amendments recently proposed and taken seriously by Congress are two that would alter the way the government raises and spends money. The proposed balanced budget amendment—which came within one vote of passage in Congress—would forbid federal outlays that exceed receipts unless three-fifths of both the House and Senate approved. The same would go for increases in the debt limit. Another proposed amendment would require a three-fifths vote for any tax increase— a requirement now in force in the House of Representatives by an internal rule. Both these amendments should be rejected, for they are both politically and economically unwise.

Fiscal supermajority amendments would depart markedly from the original constitutional scheme. If enacted into the Constitution, they would be the first amendments to abandon majority rule in ordinary legislation. The framers viewed supermajority requirements as strong medicine, to be used only in the extraordinary settings of ratifying treaties, impeaching government officers, expelling members from Congress, overriding presidential vetoes, and enacting constitutional amendments. All else was left to simple majority vote—including taxing, spending, and borrowing measures.

The framers of the Constitution considered but rejected supermajority requirements for ordinary legislation, preferring majority rule. As James Madison warned in *The Federalist* No. 58, if supermajorities were required for ordinary legislation, "it would be no longer the majority that would rule: the power would be transferred to the minority." Under the proposed fiscal supermajority amendments, that is exactly what would happen. Three-fifths of each house of Congress would be required to increase taxes or to authorize deficit spending and the increased borrowing needed to finance it. That means that two-fifths of either house of Congress could hold the budget hostage. What's wrong with that? As Madison so delicately put it, the few could extort from the many "unreasonable indulgences"—in modern parlance, pork—as the price for the additional votes needed for a supermajority. The amendments in that event would not eliminate tax increases or deficit spending but merely alter how their costs and benefits were distributed.

But if these amendments are bad for democracy, they are worse fiscal policy. The balanced budget amendment reflects alarm that the deficit grew sharply as a percentage of GNP in the 1980s and that too great a debt load is being passed on to future generations. The tax increase amendment reflects a view that government spending crowds out growth. Both these concerns are misguided.

In fact, deficit spending has saved the nation from recession and supported economic recovery time and again since World War II. Raising taxes and cutting government spending in a recession is a recipe for worsening the situation, even to the point of causing depression. Yet that is exactly what the balanced budget amendment would require Congress to do. Moreover, raising taxes in order to increase government spending can fuel growth rather than restrain it. If the balanced budget amendment had been in place and enforceable over the past half century, the nation's economic health would be a great deal weaker now.

In addition, the balanced budget amendment ignores the fact that long-term investments, whether in buildings, bombers, or education, produce benefits over their lifetimes that in the long run often exceed their costs. Unless the federal government were to separate its capital budget from its operating budget—a matter the proposed amendment has never addressed—balancing the federal budget each year would require capital investments to be paid for all at once rather than amortized gradually. No family or business operates that way. Telling the federal government to balance its total budget each year is like telling a family to pay up front for its entire mortgage in the same year it buys a house.

Finally, both the balanced budget and the tax increase amendments would alter the constitutional framework by shifting power over government spending from Congress to the president and the courts. The president might assert the power or the obligation to impound funds that Congress had authorized and appropriated. Even the potential for impoundment would give the president the leverage for arm-twisting in Congress. Like minority holdouts in the Congress, the president might have an incentive not so much to decrease spending as to redirect the distribution of any cuts away from his own favorite projects. And both amendments are engraved invitations to taxpayers to file lawsuits objecting to measures that they claim increase their taxes or to any expenditures said to unbalance the budget. Taxpayers normally do not have standing to come into court to complain about how the government is run—except when a specific constitutional provision specifically limits congressional power to tax and spend. The proposed fiscal amendments could give whole new meaning to that exception, drawing unelected judges deeply into matters of economic policy.

All this tinkering with the framers' handiwork might be worthwhile if it were necessary or likely to work, but it is neither. It is unnecessary because politics—ordinary politics—is sufficient to pressure the government to maintain tax levels or to reduce the deficit if that is the soundest course. Deficit reduction by the president and Congress during the first Clinton administration proved as much. What matters to the nation's economic health is whether the deficit is growing faster than GNP—which it has not been—not whether there is a deficit in the abstract. Congress is in the best position to make this determination without the artificial constraint of a constitutional amendment.

The proposed fiscal amendments are likely to be futile in any event because end runs around them are so easy. A balanced budget amendment is less likely to eliminate deficit spending than to drive it underground. For example, Congress could manipulate the "estimates" on which a "balanced budget" is based, could shift taxing and spending "off budget" to quasi-public entities, or could transfer costs to the states through unfunded mandates. States with balanced budget requirements have long used similar financial gimmicks. For example, they have shifted expenses to off-budget accounts, accelerated receipts and delayed expenditures, and engaged in repeated borrowing against the same assets in order to close their budget gaps. Many of them fail to eliminate deficits anyway, despite their constitutional mandates. This is so even though states, unlike the federal government, have the benefit of running separate capital and operating budgets.

As to tax increases, the devil is in the definition. Does a "tax increase" include a reduction in entitlements? A redefinition of income or the basis for calculating tax liability rather than an increase in tax rates? Such disagreements about interpretation are inevitable and cannot possibly be settled without intricate detail more typical of the Internal Revenue Code than of the Constitution.

The Constitution properly protects minorities who cannot protect themselves adequately in the normal political process. Surely we can protect our own children and grandchildren adequately without writing what might well prove an empty exhortation to do so into the Constitution.

Chapter

12

THE ITEM VETO

by Nelson W. Polsby

As of January 1997, a law has come on the books giving the president a new and unprecedented power to disallow individual items within certain legislative enactments without vetoing the entire bill. In effect, the president has by ordinary legislation been granted an item veto. It is reasonable to expect a prompt test of the constitutionality of this law, in light of a fairly recent ruling of the Supreme Court striking down the practice known as the legislative veto because that procedure introduced an irregular form of lawmaking not contemplated in the Constitution. The analogy between an item veto for the president and a legislative veto for one or more houses of Congress creates what is sure to be an irresistible basis for a constitutional challenge.

But in any event the logic supporting giving the item veto to U.S. presidents is hopelessly muddled. The idea is that with this formidable weapon presidents will prevent members of Congress from loading up appropriations bills with pork-barreling special projects, or from authorizing them in the first place. This, according to advocates of the item veto, would reduce federal expenditures and cut back on budget deficits and the national debt. A closer look reveals problems with this scenario.

Members of Congress are not alone in having or supporting special projects. Presidents have them too. An item veto would simply mean that special projects presidents like will survive, while those they dislike will not. This would transfer significant power over individual projects to the president, taking it away from Congress and its members. One would think presidents have power enough already over the pattern of allocations that the government generates, and that shared power over the location and distribution of programs is a better arrangement.

The item veto would make Congress severely dependent on presidential goodwill. A shrewd president would not veto everything but would use the item veto selectively, in effect bribing legislators into cooperating. Americans have a stake in preserving the independent judgment of Congress on issues of public policy. This is not the way to do it.

The weapon-of-the-weak left to Congress under the item veto would be embarrassment. High-profile items that a responsible Congress would never seriously propose would become attractive nuisances in the legislative process. The congressional strategy would be to let the president suffer the embarrassment of having to remove popular but too expensive items. Thus, the item veto would help legislators do what they already do so well—claim credit.

The underlying misconception is that all congressional projects amount to is a pork barrel and that these are largely responsible for budgetary deficits and the national debt. But this is untrue. Most recently, the big expenditures that put the budget out of kilter were caused by the combination of President Reagan's high-spending defense budget and his revenue-reducing tax cuts, all item-veto-proof because they were presidential rather than congressional initiatives. Before the Reagan years, our largest budget deficits were caused by the expenditures required to fight wars.

This exposes the fallacy of comparing the national government—as item veto advocates do—to those forty-odd state governments where the governor has an item veto. State governments have no defense expenditures. And most of them have weak state legislatures. Perhaps these arrangements are tolerable in political systems of intermediate size or smaller, like states, where it is easier for ordinary citizens to reach out directly and touch government to express their needs and preferences. But not so at the national level, where a strong Congress is needed for this purpose. Anything that weakens Congress weakens anybody who can get the attention of a member of Congress more readily than he or she can connect with a government bureaucracy. This includes nearly everybody, not just so-called special interests, which anyhow generally have ample capacity to lobby the executive branch.

It is simply a delusion to think that giving the president the constitutional weapon of an item veto will do away with special interests. It will protect the president's pet interests, encourage activists to make their deals with presidents, and weaken everybody's incentives to bargain with Congress. It will make members of Congress more irresponsible, giving them incentives to propose impractical measures that make them look good, and forcing the president either to veto measures that have popular appeal or risk the erosion of sound government.

Part 4

Delicate Balances

Chapter

13

LIBERTY AND COMMUNITY

by Alan Brinkley

Nothing is so central to America's image of itself as the idea of individual liberty. It is, we believe, what spurred many of the first European settlers to leave their homelands and come to our shores. It is what drove the revolutionaries who broke with England and created a new nation. It is what shaped the Constitution and, above all, the Bill of Rights. And it has been, we claim, the defining characteristic of our democracy for more than two centuries.

It is true, of course, that rights and freedoms have been central to our history and basic to our political and social system. But they have not been the only force shaping our public world. At least equally important, through most of American history, has been the idea of community.

In our present world, there is considerable anxiety about how successfully the idea of community has survived in the twentieth century and considerable criticism of the

preoccupation with rights that many critics claim has dominated (and distorted) both liberalism and conservatism in
the postwar era. This is an old complaint. Americans have
been lamenting the decline of community for centuries—
since at least the seventeenth century, when Puritan clerics
began delivering jeremiads lamenting the passing of the
close-knit religious communities of the first years of English
settlement. The laments about the decline of community
today are less theological but no less impassioned. Intellectual and popular discourse alike are filled with warnings
that the core of our life as a nation is disappearing, that we
will soon find ourselves bereft of the institutional and cultural underpinnings of a healthy society.

A growing chorus of powerful voices has emerged in
recent years—from both the left and the right—charging
that the bonds of community in the United States are dan-
gerously eroding; that the character of our civic life has
changed in ways that often seem to accentuate individual, as
opposed to community, loyalties; that we are in danger of
becoming an atomized society unable to forge vital social
bonds. Both liberalism and conservatism in our time, some
communitarian critics claim, have often tended to elevate
rights to so high a place in the lexicon of values that other,
equally important values have suffered. There is at least
some truth in these claims.

*   *   *

American liberalism for most of the past fifty years has
often seemed wedded to the idea that individual rights are
paramount, and that only in exceptional cases can a national or community interest override them. The political theorist Michael Sandel, for example, argues that liberals insist
on government remaining neutral on questions of values

and morality, on having it play no role in defining a good life or a good society because any such definition would likely favor one group's values over those of another. Citizens are autonomous—independent selves who must define their own values and goals. And government's role is to create the kind of society in which every individual can live, as far as possible, as he or she chooses. Sandel is correct, in theory at least, that liberalism in our time has espoused the ideas of individual autonomy and unfettered personal choice and that some liberals have celebrated their marriage to those concepts by pointing to dark alternatives—to the dangers inherent in more collective social orders. Indeed, to some liberal intellectuals, the idea of community has not only seemed less important than individual rights but even poses a potential threat. They have embraced an argument made particularly clear more than sixty years ago by Reinhold Niebuhr in *Moral Man and Immoral Society*. "Individual men," Niebuhr wrote,

> may be moral. . . . They are endowed by nature with a measure of sympathy and consideration for their kind. . . . Their rational faculty prompts them to a sense of justice. . . . But all these achievements are more difficult, if not impossible, for human societies and social groups. [For] In every human group there is less reason to guide and to check impulse, less capacity for self-transcendence, less ability to comprehend the needs of others and therefore more unrestrained egotism than the individuals, who compose the group, reveal in their personal relationships.

In other words, Niebuhr claims (as have some more recent liberals), liberty and even morality reside most effectively within the autonomous individual; the more the individual becomes embedded within a group (a "crowd," a "mass"), the more endangered liberty and morality become. It is on the basis of this strain—an often powerful strain—within liberalism that the communitarian critique is founded.

Much of American conservatism, despite its contempt for what liberals have done in the past half century, rests heavily on a very similar set of beliefs. Many conservatives also attribute to liberty a value far higher than they attribute to any community or collective interest; they too see the collective as not just inferior to, but as a threat to, personal freedom. Their definition of liberty rests much more heavily than the liberal definition on economic considerations: the commitment to an unregulated free market, the belief that economic freedom, as Friedrich Hayek wrote fifty years ago in *The Road to Serfdom*, is inseparable from all other notions of freedom because economic power "is the control of the means of all our ends." Whereas some liberals believe government must be neutral in its relationship to values, behavior, and social norms, many conservatives believe government must be neutral in terms of markets, economic institutions, and the distribution of personal wealth. While some liberals fear the irrationality and immorality of the "mass," some conservatives fear the tyranny of the state.

This regime of rights and freedoms—a regime supported, in different ways, by elements in both political parties and by some of the most powerful political philosophies of the past half century—has culminated, its critics charge, in a raging popular discontent with the public sphere, in a sense among many people that they have lost control of their lives, in a growing despair about the future, and in a belief that the institutions that have guided us through most of our history have somehow spent themselves. The public arena as we have known it, many have come to believe, seems now to lack the resources to answer that cry. Society yearns for something more than rights and freedom—for a sense of community capable of giving individual lives meaning, for the civic life that forms the basis for the liberty we cherish.

*   *   *

But the communitarian critique, as eloquent and compelling as it seems in the context of our present, unhappy public life, has some serious shortcomings—both as a description of politics as it is and as a prescription for politics as it should be. It is not wholly clear, first of all, that the bonds of civic life have in fact eroded as thoroughly as some critics charge. The supposed disappearance of what some communitarians (and many others) call "civil society" and others call "social capital" is almost impossible to document with any precision. Many traditional institutions of civic life have indeed weakened or vanished, but many new ones have emerged to replace them—a process that has been continuous in American society for two centuries.

Nor is it clear that either liberalism or conservatism in our time have been as wholly bound to the idea of rights as many critics claim. There are, in fact, countless examples of definitions offered by both liberals and conservatives of the "good life" and the "moral society," definitions that go far beyond a simple endorsement of personal liberty. For liberals, a wide range of social policies—housing subsidies, highway building, environmental regulations, civil rights and affirmative action, public support for the arts, and others— do, in fact, express a vision of a "good life," even if one that critics of liberalism may find insufficiently ennobling. Many liberals have gone further and endorsed ideas of national service, cooperative workplace structures, and other explicitly communitarian goals. Conservatives, too, have proposed visions of community based on a prescriptive moral agenda encompassing a wide range of behavioral norms rooted in a normative (and often religious) concept of how individuals and families should live and behave.

But the largest shortcoming of the communitarian argument is the way some of its advocates define community itself. Many (although certainly not all) contemporary communitarians consider community inseparable from localism. It is the neighborhood church, PTA, Little League, Boy or Girl Scout chapter, Elks Club, or (to use the political scientist Robert Putnam's now-famous example) bowling league that is the source of civic life. It is the local voluntary association—the sort of organization that Tocqueville argued was so characteristic of early-nineteenth-century America—that makes it possible for individuals to weave themselves into a community. Some communitarians, to be sure, see a link between the local community and the nation. They see in local civic life a vehicle for creating habits of community interaction and social trust from which a larger political community can eventually emerge. But other communitarians—those on the right in particular—envision no such links. The threat to community, they claim, is not just excessive individualism; it is also excessive centralization. The "community" stands in opposition to the "nation" or the "government." It is a defense against impersonal bureaucracies, against the state, against the larger world. And as such, they claim, it is part of a tradition deeply embedded in American history.

It is true, needless to say, that this localistic vision of community has firm roots in the American past—as the frequent evocations of Tocqueville by today's communitarians make clear. Historians and others have spent several decades exploring the tradition of what they call republicanism, a

vision of society that emerged in the eighteenth century and
survived (according to some, although not all, of its chron-
iclers) through the nineteenth and into the twentieth in various populist movements, in certain areas of the labor
movement, in some parts of the left, even in elements of the
communitarian right. The republican tradition (closely associated with, among others, Thomas Jefferson) places a high
value on personal liberty, to be sure, but it situates liberty
within the fabric of a relatively small and homogeneous
community whose citizens operate according to a shared
moral code and a respect for social norms.

What gives rights and freedoms meaning? Many liberals and libertarians would argue that their meaning is inherent, that they are themselves the foundation of our public
world. But republicans would argue differently. Liberty has
no meaning except in a social context; rights cannot be sustained unless there is a civic life healthy enough to create a
shared commitment to them. Communities create freedom;
freedom does not create itself. But in order to create freedom, communities also create obligations—obligations to
honor certain common values, to respect certain institutions, to accept some common definition of what is good.
We cannot hope to be truly free, according to the tradition
of republicanism, unless we identify with and participate
in the governance of the political community upon which
our freedom depends. And we can only do so, many republicans have argued throughout American history, if the
community remains small enough that individuals can realistically expect to exercise some power within it.

The historian and social critic Christopher Lasch, in one
of his last books, *The True and Only Heaven*, drew particular attention to today's close-knit, ethnically homogeneous,
working-class communities as examples of healthy, vibrant
societies. Lasch was deeply disheartened by the condition of

modern middle-class life—by what he considered its heedless
materialism, its resistance to social bonds, its rejection of
obligation to family and neighborhood, its transformation of
individuals into isolated, self-regarding, narcissistic beings.
The Italian or Irish or Jewish or other ethnic neighborhoods
of many American cities, with their strong family and community bonds, seemed to him a model for what the rest of
society might become. And it is true that there is much to
admire in close and enduring ties of family and church and
neighborhood, in the sense of mutual obligation that characterizes many such communities. A healthy society depends
on tight families, vibrant neighborhoods, healthy schools
and churches and fraternal societies—thriving patterns of
local association. Those things are the foundations of community. Without them, the forces in modern society that
atomize individuals would be impossible to withstand.

But Lasch's example also reveals the problem of basing
our hopes for community entirely on local, family- and
neighborhood-centered structures. The United States is a
vast nation of remarkable diversity, and its most difficult
dilemma throughout its history has been finding a way for
so many different kinds of people, and so many different
kinds of communities, to live together peacefully and productively. That dilemma has become even more perplexing
in the twentieth century, as a modern industrial economy
and a pervasive mass culture have made it virtually impossible for any group to live in isolation from the larger world.
A purely local vision of community is, today at least, a prescription not for harmony but for balkanization and conflict.
The tight-knit ethnic communities Lasch celebrates may have
many virtues, but they can also be (and have often been)
places where bigotry flourishes and interracial violence erupts.
Other kinds of insular communities seem at least equally
hostile to any notion of a stable, tolerant society: the gated,

affluent communities that are now spreading across our landscape, based on an understandable fear of crime, to be sure, but an ominous sign of the fragmentation of our nation; the armed cults and militias, which have become visible to us only relatively recently, setting themselves up in opposition (at times violent opposition) to government and mainstream society; some, although by no means all, of the militant Christian communities, which attempt to impose a rigid religious orthodoxy on unwilling neighbors; and many others. A society whose principal conception of community is small, insular groups clinging to traditional bonds is a society on the road to profound conflict and division.

*   *   *

But there is also a larger vision of community, with equally strong roots in American history. The kind of community that forms the basis of a stable, healthy society—particularly a society as vast and diverse as ours—transcends localism and parochialism. It rests as much on a concept of the nation as it does on that of neighborhood, or town, or region. This idea of a national community is, in fact, among the oldest and most powerful in our history—at least as old and as powerful as the republican ideal with which it sometimes seems to compete. It is the source of our Constitution and the basis of the most powerful political traditions of the first century of our nation's existence.

The framers of the Constitution wanted, of course, to protect liberty. They wanted to create a form of government that would ensure the rights of the individual. But they understood, too, that liberty could be secured only in a large political community, a genuine nation. At the Constitutional Convention in Philadelphia (according to James Madison's diaries), Alexander Hamilton "confessed that he was much

discouraged by the amazing extent of the Country in expect-
ing the desired blessings from any general sovereignty that
could be substituted." How, he asked, could a government
effectively unite such a vast and diverse nation? Hamilton
was expressing a widely shared fear, expressed most promi-
nently by the French political theorist Montesquieu and
understood throughout the English-speaking world. Popular
government, Montesquieu had warned, could not function
within a large country; such a government would be torn
apart by "a thousand private views" and would lead to
attempts at despotism by ambitious leaders.

But James Madison offered an answer to Hamilton and
Montesquieu—an answer that Hamilton ultimately embraced
and that became the heart of the American national idea.
The size and diversity of the nation, Madison wrote in *The
Federalist* No. 10, was in fact the best hope for stability.
The greatest danger to a healthy society was "faction": "a
number of citizens . . . who are united and actuated by
some common impulse of passion or of interest, adverse
to the rights of other citizens, or to the permanent and
aggregate interests of the community." How could a society avoid the plague of faction? There were two ways, he
argued. One was "removing the causes of faction," a dangerous course because it would involve either destroying
liberty or enforcing a uniformity of views—both of which
would be remedies "worse than the disease." The other
was "controlling [the] effects" of faction. And to do that,
he claimed, required a large political community in which
every faction, no matter how large, would have to deal
with and accommodate others. "A pure Democracy,"
Madison wrote, "by which I mean, a Society consisting of
a small number of citizens, who assemble and administer
the Government in person, can admit of no cure for the
mischiefs of faction." The solution to faction lay in an

extensive republic, spanning a vast and diverse country, where no one faction could prevail.

President Washington, in his 1796 Farewell Address (largely written by Hamilton), similarly stressed the importance of a strong union as the framework for a workable national community. The Union was not a mere staging ground upon which factions could do battle. Nor was it simply a strong central government capable of tempering local passions. It was a state of mind—a commitment of citizens to each other and to a common sense of purpose and obligation, "an indissoluble community of interest as one nation." Washington, Madison, Hamilton, and the other founders of our nation had great respect for the small communities that bounded the lives of most citizens. But they understood, too, that for America to survive and flourish, there had to be a larger idea of community as well.

Their idea was not uncontested. Jefferson for a time offered a partial dissent, in his vision of a small, agrarian republic united by the commonality of interest and sentiment of its citizens rather than by the power of a strong national political community. But as president he gradually moved away from his agrarian visions and presided over a significant increase in both the extent and the unity of the nation. A more serious challenge came in the mid-nineteenth century from the American South. "The very idea of an American People, as constituting a single community, is a mere chimera," John C. Calhoun once said. "Such a community never for a moment existed." The Civil War was, among other things, a battle to defeat Calhoun's idea. Daniel Webster based his famous defenses of the Union on the idea that the survival of liberty depended on the survival of a national community—"Liberty and Union, one and inseparable, now and forever." There was, he insisted, a "common good" that transcended local interests, a partnership based in part on economic interest but also in part on spiritual union. One of the great admirers of Webster's words was Abraham Lincoln.

The concept of a national community met a challenge again in the late nineteenth and early twentieth centuries, with the rise of large-scale industrial capitalism and the enormous social and economic dislocations that accompanied it. Laissez-faire capitalism—and such intellectual rationales for it as Social Darwinism—celebrated individual initiative, the "survival of the fittest," and the value of acquisitive individualism as the basis of society. Everyone ultimately benefited from the achievements of talented, successful people, the Social Darwinists claimed. Constraining their activities in the interests of the "community" would be to retard the healthy progress of society.

The populists offered one answer to laissez-faire. Economic growth that eroded communities and the autonomy of individuals was, they insisted, both unfair and unnecessary. The economy could grow and prosper in a more humane way, through a network of smaller-scale institutions rooted in communities, but also through the intervention of a powerful national government holding industrialists, financiers, and in the end everyone to a higher standard than maximizing profit. The local communities the populists were fighting to preserve could not survive, they believed, without a national community capable of restraining private power and protecting the interests of ordinary people.

Another response to laissez-faire came from progressive reformers, among them Theodore Roosevelt, a champion of industrial growth and economic progress but also a staunch defender of the idea of "the solidarity, the essential unity of our [national community]." The modern world had unleashed great forces, Roosevelt recognized, forces that had enormous capacity to do good, to create progress. But that progress would be for naught if it came at the cost of the dignity of individuals and the vitality of communities. Individuals and local communities were powerless by themselves to withstand the assaults of modern, large-scale organizations. Only a national community—embodied, Roosevelt believed, in a vigorous democratic state—would make it possible for local communities, and the individual liberty dependent on them, to survive. "I believe in corporations," Roosevelt once said. "They are indispensable instruments of our modern civilization; but I believe that they should be so supervised and so regulated that they shall act for the interest of the community as a whole." The health of the nation depended on the "capacity to subordinate the interests of the individual to the interests of the community," and the realization of that capacity depended on national standards and national power.

The New Deal is remembered, and often excoriated, today as the source of contemporary liberalism and its supposed preoccupation with rights and entitlements. It did, of course, contribute in critical ways to the creation of the rights-based liberalism that has been so much in evidence in the last half century. But the New Deal was also deeply committed to the concept of community—both to the restoration of local communities and to the strengthening of the overarching national community. From the beginning of his administration, Franklin Roosevelt's rhetoric was suffused with images of nationhood, of interdependence, of community. (In his first inaugural address, he never once used the words "liberty," "individual," or "equality.") The early New Deal was, above all else, an effort to find concepts of community capable of transcending the bitter struggles dividing groups in the economy and the society from one another. The New Deal's first major effort at economic reform, the

National Recovery Administration, tried (although it ultimately failed) to create what New Dealers called "cooperative action among trade groups," to define a "community of
interest" that would draw together capital, labor, government, and the consumer. It was an effort to temper the bru-
tality of the industrial economy, to insist on national
standards of "community interest" amid the harsh, competitive struggle of capitalism.

Many of those impulses ultimately faded from New
Deal thought, and others—which focused more intently on
rights and entitlements—emerged to replace them, so that
postwar liberalism had a weaker connection with the idea of
community than most of the progressive and reform traditions that preceded it. Postwar conservatism, too, in its preoccupation with delegitimizing the New Deal and opposing
communism, elevated the idea of liberty to a more central
place than it had ever occupied before. The present popular
discontent with the public sphere is in part a result of that
postwar decline in community sentiment. Certainly those
who lament the passing of community and yearn for its
revival have found contemporary political discourse barren
of language and ideas capable of satisfying them.

*   *   *

These small chapters in the history of ideas of community in
America, therefore, resonate with questions that preoccupy
our own time. History teaches us, we hear from many quar-
ters (including, at times, the halls of Congress and the bench
of the Supreme Court), that a strong national community
and a powerful federal government are artificial accretions
of modern liberalism, incompatible with our traditions and
our values. But history teaches no such thing. Our traditions and our values have never been fixed or uniform; they

have always included—in addition to a strong commitment to individual rights and personal freedoms—a powerful sense of the value of community and the importance of the nation.

The political world of today is preoccupied with divisions and oppositions: the government versus the market; the national versus the local; the public versus the private; liberty versus community. The rhetoric of our time asks us to choose among these conflicting values and ideas—to accept that we can have one but not the other. But the history of our nation's political traditions suggests that these divisions are entirely artificial, that it is unnecessary to choose. Indeed, it is not just unnecessary but destructive. We need a vigorous government and a healthy market. We need strong national institutions and strong local ones. We need a healthy public sector and a healthy private one. Above all, perhaps, we need—to paraphrase Webster—liberty and community, for neither is sustainable without the other.

Chapter

14

REPRESENTATION OF RACIAL MINORITIES

by Kathleen M. Sullivan

How are minorities to be protected from oppression by the majority? One way is to invalidate any legislative outcome that burdens them excessively by enforcing constitutional rights. Government may not, for example, censor dissident political minorities, persecute unorthodox religious minorities, discriminate against racial minorities, or level the property of the richest few by uncompensated takings or impairments of contract. Such rights place minority interests beyond the reach of politics; they amount to judicially enforced exemptions from majority rule. An alternative approach is to ensure that minorities are well represented in legislative processes from the start. The Senate, for example, gives disproportionate representation to geographical minorities from small states. Other minorities have gained representation through expansion of the franchise: the right to vote, once the province of propertied white men, was guaranteed to all men twenty-one or older by the Fourteenth Amendment, to African-Americans by the Fifteenth, to women by the Nineteenth, to persons too poor to pay a poll tax by the Twenty-fourth, and to all persons eighteen or older by the Twenty-sixth. Formal voting power ensures that none of these minorities—or, in the case of women, a traditionally disempowered majority—can be excluded altogether from political decisions affecting their fate.

But what if formal enfranchisement and rights against discriminatory outcomes are not enough? That has been the situation with representation of racial minorities in Congress. The Reconstruction amendments decreed an end to denial of the vote on account of race. To be formally included in governance, however, is not necessarily to be substantively effective. The Voting Rights Act of 1965 recognized as much and sought to launch a second Reconstruction. The act outlawed various abusive practices by white majorities that had deterred the formal exercise of voting rights by blacks. But it recognized that the problem ran deeper—that it was structural. Even assuming robust turnout in voting, racial minorities can still lack influence in legislative outcomes. The problem is not simply that they are by definition outnumbered. It is also that they are unable to forge alliances with other groups in the political process adequate to protect their interests. As Justice Harlan Fiske Stone once put it, "prejudice against discrete and insular minorities may be a special condition, which tends seriously to curtail the operation of those political processes ordinarily to be relied upon to protect minorities." Political minorities are normally expected to find allies in politics or else to take their lumps. But under conditions of racial bloc voting, lumps will be forthcoming; allies will not.

Viewing race as impervious to the usual give-and-take of politics, the Voting Rights Act tried to ensure that black Americans would get to elect at least some candidates of their choice. The principle has since been extended to other racial minorities, especially Hispanic voters. In local elections, for example, the act spurred the creation of district-based elections to replace at-large elections to multimember bodies that had stubbornly remained all-white. A racial minority systematically outnumbered in an at-large system might elect representatives from among its own number in a smaller district in which it had majority control.

Along similar lines, the act has influenced the way that congressional districts are drawn. Nothing in the Constitution requires states to use districts to elect members of the House of Representatives; they are charged simply with determining the "time, place and manner" of federal elections, subject to congressional override. But all states have divided themselves into districts for this purpose, beginning in the earliest days of the Republic. District lines have not been drawn simply by algorithm or disembodied mapmakers but by an intensely political process that takes several variables into account.

First, attention is paid to traditional local jurisdictional boundaries and the preservation of preexisting communities. Second, districts have customarily been drawn with an eye to "compactness and contiguity"—they are not supposed to sprawl all over the state. Since 1964, the Supreme Court has imposed a third criterion that often generates some tension with the first two: each district must contain an equal population because the constitutional requirement of equal protection, as the Court interpreted it, entails "one person, one vote." But there are a large number of ways that a state might draw the lines dividing equipopulous districts. In choosing particular lines, state legislatures have paid respect to a fourth set of considerations: partisan advantage and incumbent protection. Such political gerry-mandering is rarely deemed an unconstitutional denial of equal protection to the other side.

Against this backdrop, the Voting Rights Act interject-ed a fifth consideration: that district lines be drawn in such a way as to remedy past discrimination against racial minori-ties that has caused them to be politically underrepresented. Thus, state legislatures, particularly in the South, have delib-erately created a number of "majority-minority" congres-sional districts, whether under court order or preemptively on their own. The results have been dramatic: between the 1990 census and the 1994 elections, the number of black members of the House of Representatives more than dou-bled, from seventeen to thirty-nine. Of those thirty-nine members, only three were elected from districts that were not majority-minority. Like one-person-one-vote, majority-minority districts often involve trade-offs with the criteria of compactness, contiguity, and conformity with traditional local boundaries. Where black voting population is diffusely distributed, such districts often have a highly irregular shape.

Majority-minority districts have come under sharp attack in recent years. Some critics have deemed them uncomfortably close to racial apartheid, notwithstanding that their intent is to empower rather than subjugate blacks. Like opponents of affirmative action in employment and education, these critics suggest that voting should be color-blind, that race-based districting reinforces racial divisions in society, and that racism can be undone only when white majorities send minorities to Congress. Others have sug-gested that racially drawn districts defeat their own purpose of increasing minority influence in politics. Concentrating minority voters in safe districts may succeed in getting minority candidates elected, they say, but it does not increase minorities' ability to enact their policy preferences into law. That is because an increase in minority concentration in one district decreases minority presence in other districts. Representatives from the remaining districts, now "bleached" of black or Hispanic votes, can safely ignore minority interests, as they need not reach out to the minority electorate. They will have no incentive, for example, to join coalitions in Congress favoring civil rights. Black and Hispanic representatives elected from safe districts will be isolated once in Congress. It would be better, say the critics, for minority voters to be spread across a number of districts in each of which they will constitute a sizable non-majority bloc to be reckoned with, or even represent the crucial swing vote in a close contest. On this view, racial districting is better for minority officeholders than for their constituents and ironically benefits whites and Republicans more than it benefits minorities and Democrats.

The critics have prevailed in several recent Supreme Court decisions interpreting the equal protection clause to bar the use of race as the predominant concern in the drawing of district lines. These decisions, like those narrowing the scope of permissible affirmative action programs, presume that race is constitutionally irrelevant to the distribution of governmental benefits as well as harms. The fate of majority-minority districts now rests on a single vote: four justices of the Supreme Court would strike down virtually all such districts, four justices would uphold virtually all such districts unless they diluted white votes (that is, unless the proportion of majority-minority districts exceeded the percentage of the minority voting population in the state), and the deciding vote belongs to Justice Sandra Day O'Connor, who would strike down only those race-based districts that are unusually bizarrely shaped, disregarding traditional districting principles such as compactness and contiguity. Race-based districts shaped like a "bug splat," the "mark of Zorro," or a "Mayan sacred bird" will fare poorly under this test, though equally race-based but neater quadrilateral districts may survive.

The critics of race-based districting, including the Supreme Court justices who have voted to strike down such districts, make some powerful arguments. But there are more powerful arguments in reply. First and most broadly, the equal protection clause nowhere mandates that all laws should be color-blind even if the electorate is not. The guarantee of equal protection is better read, in light of its history, to protect against the imposition of racial disadvantage, not against all advertence to race. A white voter suffers no injury on the basis of race if he or she lands in a majority-minority district, so long as the strength of his or her vote is not diluted—so long as such districts are not numerically disproportionate to the percentage of the minority voting population. Absent dilution, it is not an injury to have to vote in a district dominated by members of another race; if it were, racial minorities in predominantly white districts would have a great many more causes for action.

Second, it is not clear that majority-minority districts perversely benefit whites and Republicans, as the critics claim. Republicans have not made greater percentage gains in the House since 1990 than in the Senate or in governorships, where elections are statewide rather than by district. Nor is it clear that black influence is greater where black votes are deconcentrated and spread across predominantly white constituencies. Democrats elected from majority-white districts in the South receive a disproportionately large share of black votes but do not vote in like degree for the civil rights agenda. Black support for white Democrats in the South might well have more to do with allegiance to the national Democratic party, which has been strongly identified with civil rights since 1964, than with any particular responsiveness on the part of these representatives.

Third, it is too soon to declare the death of racially polarized voting. The critics emphasize that a number of black representatives have been elected to Congress from districts that are not majority-black—including, in the 1996 elections, five incumbent black representatives who had originally won election from majority-black districts that were redrawn in response to constitutional challenges. These reelections, of course, are occasions for some optimism. But the picture is more complicated than the critics make out. To begin with, it is hardly apparent that these incumbents would ever have been elected to their first terms, and thus gained the considerable advantages of incumbency, if they had had to run initially in their districts as newly configured rather than in the original, majority-black districts that were later struck down. In Georgia, for example, the two black incumbents received only 31 percent and 36 percent of the white votes in their reconfigured districts. Moreover, in several of the redrawn districts where black incumbents won reelection, whites remained a minority: the two redrawn Texas districts were 44 percent black and 21 percent Hispanic in one case and 42 percent black and 16 percent Hispanic in the other in 1996. One cannot conclude from these reelections, therefore, that the days of white backlash against black candidates or constituencies are over. Black mayors elected in cities in which black voters are less than a majority are similarly often elected by multiracial coalitions, not by color-blind white majorities.

For these reasons, the Supreme Court should not strike down every majority-minority district that comes before it. In the end, the debate between the critics and defenders of majority-minority districts turns on conceptions of representation. Which is better for a constituency with distinctive interests: some influence over many legislators or decisive influence over a few? Both sides agree that representative government must entail some meaningful power sharing among groups, so long as groups have different and often mutually antagonistic interests. But they disagree over the means. The critics say that racial minorities are better off seeking to assert their influence as nonmajority voting blocs diffused within the polity. The defenders say that the interests of minority voters are better served by strongly committed representatives seeking to assert their influence as legislators within the Congress. The defenders have the better of the argument. On the framers' theory, representatives would take into account various interests and through disinterested deliberation arrive at a public consensus that mediates between them. At the end of the twentieth century, the intransigence of racial polarization suggests that the interests of minorities will be better taken into account if some minority representatives are themselves present in the room.

Chapter

15

THE BALANCE OF POWER BETWEEN THE FEDERAL GOVERNMENT AND THE STATES

by Kathleen M. Sullivan

T he antifederalists opposed the Constitution out of fear that it would give too much power to the federal government. Contemporary antifederalists claim their intellectual ancestors were right, and they seek to roll federal power back in a variety of ways. Governors and new members of Congress ally to devolve welfare policy to the fifty states. State and local law enforcement officers refuse to perform the background checks on handgun purchasers required by the federal Brady law in order to keep guns out of criminal hands. State motor vehicle bureaus try to resist a federal "motor voter" law requiring them to offer to register citizens to vote at the same time as they license them to drive. Criminal defendants, newly emboldened as states' rights advocates, argue that Congress lacks power to regulate local crimes. Governors seek legislation providing that Congress will pay for any mandates with which it might burden the states.

These modern antifederalists invoke the structure of the Constitution, which gave limited powers to the federal government, and the text of the Tenth Amendment, which reiterated that all other powers were reserved to the states. On the antifederalists' view, the peoples of the various states, not "We the People of the United States," are the ultimate source of constitutional authority. They argue that "We the People" have engaged in a power grab, tilting the balance of power too far in favor of the federal government. They demand that the courts should right that balance, as Congress is unlikely to restrain itself. In short, they have developed a modern ideology of states' "rights" against federal laws.

The framers of the Constitution would hardly recognize such an ideology. In their view, the Constitution was not a winner-take-all contest for sovereignty between the federal government and the states. It sought instead, in Justice Anthony Kennedy's words, to "split the atom of sovereignty" in two. The United States is neither a centralized nation-state like France nor a loose confederation of independent, sovereign entities like the European Union. Rather, it is what Madison called a "compound republic": "We the People of the United States" ordained the Constitution, but it was ratified only by the consent of the peoples of the several states. And while it strengthened the federal government, the Constitution contemplated a robust state governmental role.

Thus, in our constitutional system, the question of state versus federal power is not a question of "rights." States do not have rights as individuals do. Nor is it a question of inviolable principles. It is instead a practical question: what allocation of power between the states and the federal government best serves our ends? In the framers' view, the federal system served two ends: liberty and the public good. People would be freer, they predicted, under two levels of government rather than just one. In *The Federalist* No. 51, for example, Madison argued that the division of power between "two distinct governments" would allow the state and federal governments to check each other, providing security to the "rights of the people." The framers also reasoned that each level of government has distinctive contributions to make to the public good. The states are better at some things; the federal government at others. The trick is to allocate responsibility for the right things to the appropriate level of government.

In their pursuit of states' "rights," modern antifederalists lose sight of the important reasons why some policies are better handled at the federal level. To begin with, the federal government is better at providing public goods whose benefits transcend state boundaries. The best example is national defense. Missiles siloed in Texas will also protect the citizens of Connecticut and California from attack by a foreign enemy. The other states might be happy to let Texas pay for the missiles itself since they would then get the benefits of protection without the cost. But in that case, Texas might well not furnish the missiles in the first place, as it would not want to give the rest of the nation a free ride. Thus, as Hamilton pointed out in *The Federalist* No. 25, only the federal government can be relied upon to provide the level of defense needed for the entire nation. Because enemies "encircle the union from Maine to Georgia," he wrote, the common danger ought to be defended against by "a common treasury," lest "the security of all . . . be subjected to the parsimony, improvidence or inability of a part."

The same argument holds true for many other public goods that benefit broad segments of the national population and hence are likely to be underproduced by any individual state. For example, the federal government provides, through federal taxation and borrowing, for interstate highways, national parks, space exploration, the Post Office, the Coast Guard, air traffic control, and the bulk of medical research, to name a few. Some have suggested that some of these goods would be provided more efficiently by private businesses than by government, but such arguments for privatization offer no support for devolution to the states.

The federal government also has a distinct advantage over the states in policing goods, persons, and businesses that move across state lines. For that reason, the Constitution makes explicit Congress's power to regulate "interstate commerce." Federal laws ensure, for example, that apple juice shipped across the country is safe to drink, that offers of securities on national markets rest on truthful information, and that deadbeat dads cannot evade one state's child-support obligations by moving to another.

Federal intervention may also be called for when an activity in one state causes more harm to residents of other states than to its own residents. For example, a state with coal-burning industries might not take adequate account of the cost of acid rain caused by their pollution in states downwind. A tobacco-growing state might downplay the health care costs associated with smoking nationwide. Interstate agreements are one solution, but the political obstacles to such bargains are often daunting. In cases like these, setting policy at the national level can break the logjam.

Federal action can also correct the problem of "races to the bottom" among the states. Each state has an interest in attracting the rich, who will pay taxes and create employment, and deflecting the poor, who will impose net costs. Thus each state has an incentive to compete with other states to attract businesses by relaxing regulations that would otherwise be in their citizens' best interests. Each state likewise has an incentive to avoid becoming a "welfare magnet" by reducing its level of social services below those offered by competing states, even if its citizens would prefer to be more generous. Any agreement among a few states to do otherwise is likely to be undercut by others. National programs or minimum federal standards can stop such destructive competition. Child labor laws, Social Security, and unemployment insurance are some examples that originated with the New Deal.

Finally, there are enormous disparities in wealth and income among the states, and only the federal government can effectively collect revenue and redistribute it from rich states to poor. A state too poor to fund minimally equipped schools, or a state that has been hit by a sudden disaster— earthquake, fire, hurricane, tornado, or flood—will be grateful for federal education aid or federal emergency relief subsidized by the citizens of other states.

What is left for the state governments to do? Almost anything they wish. As Madison noted in *The Federalist* No. 45, while federal powers are "few and defined," the powers of the states "are numerous and indefinite." Although the enumerated federal powers have of course been construed more expansively than the framers anticipated, the powers of the states remain unbounded in scope and variety. So long as they do not enter into treaties, coin money, grant titles of nobility, pass bills of attainder, ex post facto laws, or laws impairing obligations of contract, or violate individual rights, states may regulate the health, safety, morals, and well-being of their citizens any way they see fit, subject only to their own state constitutions.

True, federal law is supreme over state law, and so Congress can preempt the states from enacting regulations that conflict with federal law. Modern antifederalists chafe at this federal supremacy. But they exaggerate the extent to which the federal government has displaced state policy-making. There are strong structural, political, and cultural limits on federalization.

First, the federal government can never set a ceiling for state policies; it can only set a floor. A state that wants to have more protection for individual liberties than the federal Constitution provides is free so to interpret its state constitution. A state that wants to have cleaner air than federal pollution standards require is not prevented from imposing stricter emission controls. Under uniform, national, minimal education standards, local school administrators could still set more ambitious performance goals. There is thus a structural limit to how far the federal government could homogenize the nation even if it wanted to.

Second, there are political limits on federalization. The state and local governments are a powerful lobbying force in their own right. They have proved capable of defending themselves politically when Congress steps too hard on their toes. For example, when the Supreme Court, reversing its own earlier states' rights ruling, upheld a federal statute telling municipalities how much to pay their police and fire-fighters, the National League of Cities and its allies persuaded Congress to rewrite the law. Such state and local governmental exemptions from generally applicable federal statutes are commonplace. Moreover, various federal legislative initiatives originate with state and local government lobbies, from the welfare policy prescriptions of the National Governors' Council to the requests of state and local law enforcement organizations for greater federal funding of community police.

Finally, federalism is rooted in long tradition. Even if it is no longer true, as Madison once wrote, that "the first and most natural attachment of the people will be to the governments of their respective States," state identity remains a powerful part of our political culture. We never vote as members of an undifferentiated national electorate. We never go to a federal polling place or vote in a nation-wide referendum. We vote for our federal representatives in the time, place, and manner set up by our state governments. We elect two senators from every state, giving small states a disproportionate voice in national governance. And we vote for the president state by state through the electoral college rather than directly by popular vote. In such a system, the president and Congress ignore distinctive state concerns at their peril.

This tradition survives because it makes practical sense to leave many policy matters to the states. To the extent that conditions vary among states, decentralized approaches can tailor policy to local circumstance. To the extent that preferences vary among states, decentralization fosters liberty. If citizens of one state feel tyrannized by its policies, they can vote with their feet by migrating freely across state lines. Hence the concentration of Mormons in Utah, libertarians in New Hampshire, environmentalists in Oregon, or gay people in northern California. Even if the states share similar goals, they may act as what Justice Louis Brandeis called "laboratories for experiment," competing with one another to develop the best means for realizing social or economic policy. The more experiments, the greater the likelihood of a breakthrough, and if one state makes a breakthrough, others can follow suit. For example, Massachusetts pioneered innovations in elementary and secondary education, California in public higher education, Wisconsin in industrial compensation and unemployment insurance, New

York in community policing, and Hawaii in universal health care, to name a few.

These structural, political, and cultural safeguards of federalism can be expected to protect state interests from the bottom up without frequent resort to judicial intervention or constitutional command. Of course, the courts should stand by to protect the states against any extreme federal incursions on their sovereignty: Congress could not tell a state where to locate its capital or how many chambers its legislature should have. It also makes sense for the courts to police outright federal intervention in state lawmaking, just as they police transgressions of the separation of powers among the federal branches.

It one illustrative case, the Supreme Court has held that Congress may not order a state either to pass laws regulating disposal of low-level radioactive waste or else to take title to the waste itself. As Justice Sandra Day O'Connor wrote for the Court, such a federal law wrongly "commandeers" the state's legislative process. If Congress passes the buck to the states to solve a national problem, she explained, "state officials may bear the brunt of public disapproval" while federal lawmakers enjoy a free ride. Lines of electoral accountability are blurred; voters will not know which set of bums to throw out.

However sensible this principle might be, modern antifederalists exaggerate its reach. Some local sheriffs claim that the federal Brady law, which requires them to run background checks on handgun purchasers, "makes the states dance like marionettes on the fingers of the federal government," in Justice Antonin Scalia's words. But requiring local law enforcement officers to inspect state arrest records does not trench upon state legislative sovereignty. Congress has made all the hard policy choices on handgun control in the Brady law and bears the brunt of any public disapproval.

When the local sheriff performs a background check, he or she is not being forced to make any policy judgments on behalf of the state. If a handgun purchaser does not like the background check, it is clear that Congress, not the sheriff, is to blame. For these reasons, the sheriffs' invocation of states' rights should be rejected.

Finally, there may be reason for the courts to draw outer limits to federal power when the structural, political, and cultural safeguards of federalism break down and the federal government encroaches needlessly upon areas traditionally and sensibly regulated by the states. The worst example in our recent politics is the overfederalization of crime. The Constitution names only three federal crimes: counterfeiting coin or securities, piracy on the high seas, and treason. But Congress has created more than three thousand federal crimes under the power to regulate interstate commerce. There are many crimes that should be federal, such as bombing federal buildings or sending explosives through the mail. But should it also be a federal crime to grow marijuana at home or to hijack a car around the corner? Federal crimes have proliferated not because it is good crime policy but because it is good politics: as Chief Justice William Rehnquist has observed, "the political combination of creating a federal offense and attaching a mandatory minimum sentence has become a veritable siren song for Congress," loud enough to drown out any careful consideration of the comparative advantages of state and federal crime control.

Shifting crime control from the states to the federal government in purely local cases diverts the work of federal investigators, prosecutors, and judges from areas of greater federal need. It also fills federal prisons with nonviolent and first-time offenders who occupy space that could better be used for violent, career criminals whose operations cross state lines. There is no reason why most of the new federal crimes could not be handled by the states, as they have been traditionally, unless they involve multistate enterprises or intrastate enterprises so vast as to overwhelm the resources of state authorities.

For such reasons, the Supreme Court recently struck down an act of Congress criminalizing possession of a handgun at school. Possession is not commerce, the gun had not been shown to have traveled across state lines, and education and crime control are traditional local functions, held the Court. Congress's power over interstate commerce is broad, but not so broad as to amount to a national police power. The Court in effect directed Congress to consider the relative merits of state and local governance before legislating—an appropriate and not excessive burden.

Contemporary antifederalists are mistaken, however, when they read this decision as a declaration of open season on federal law. Some courts have invalidated federal laws against rape and other violence against women. Others have invalidated federal laws making it a crime to fail to pay child support. These laws, though, involve subjects quite different from gun possession at school. Stopping sexual and other battery of women may not implicate interstate commerce, but it may well implicate Congress's power to enforce federal civil rights. Congress has long had expansive power not only to stop invidious discrimination in the states but also to eliminate conditions in which it might flourish. While it is a close question, a high incidence of private violence against women might amount to such a regulable condition. Child-support evasion is an easier case, for it involves a classic problem warranting federal intervention, the problem of mobility across state lines. In enacting both these laws, unlike the gun possession law, Congress paid more than lip service to the balance of federal and state power.

Against this backdrop, there is little warrant for an antifederalist revival. If power has flowed to the center since the nation's founding, that is in large part because federal power has served as a crucial check on local factionalism and as a source of ingenious solutions to coordination problems among the states. To the extent that imbalance of state and federal power is a problem, it is largely self-correcting because the states can protect themselves through politics. To the extent that it is not, the Supreme Court has supplied sensible but narrow outer limits. There is no need for greater judicial intervention on the states' behalf.

Chapter

16

RELEGITIMIZING GOVERNMENT

by Alan Brinkley

In the early years of the twentieth century, as Americans confronted the enormous social changes industrialization had imposed on their world, a great project slowly emerged that would capture much of the national imagination for at least eight decades. The project grew out of the strong and growing faith among many Americans in the capacity of society to impose order and rational purpose on the conduct of national affairs. And it envisioned, among other things, a new and greatly expanded role for the federal government— which through most of its existence to that point had been a relatively weak and insignificant force in the life of the nation—in countering the growth of concentrated private power and providing a central intelligence through which society could right itself and plan effectively for the future.

Walter Lippmann, in his 1915 book *Drift and Mastery*, expressed this faith in the possibility of creating an intelligent control of the great forces of modernity—a faith that he himself would soon repudiate—as clearly as anyone else of his time. "In the last thirty years or so," he wrote, "We know that the huge corporation, the integrated industry, production for a world market, the network of combinations, pools, and agreements have played havoc with the older political economy. The scope of human endeavor is enormously larger, and with it has come . . . a general change of social scale. Human thought has had to enlarge its scale in order to meet the situation." Older patterns of thought, Lippmann stated with considerable disdain, could not keep up with the new forces of modern society. They produced aimlessness, drift. "Mankind," he lamented, "lives today only in the intervals of a fitful sleep." The alternative to drift—for individuals and for nations—was what Lippmann called "mastery . . . the substitution of conscious intention for unconscious striving. Civilization, it seems to me, is just this constant effort to introduce plan where there has been clash, and purpose into the jungles of disordered growth."

Lippmann's faith in the dream of "mastery"—his belief in the urgency of introducing "plan where there has been clash"—rested on two related assumptions, both of which have survived (with varying degrees of hardiness) into our own time. One was descriptive: a belief that the most powerful force of history in the modern, industrial age was the drive toward consolidation, centralization, bureaucratization. This was an idea introduced, to the intellectual world at least, by the German sociologist Ferdinand Tonnies in 1887 in his book *Gemeinschaft und Gesellschaft,* and later refined and expanded by Max Weber. More recently it has been adopted by influential groups of scholars who have promoted what some have called modernization theory and others the "organizational thesis," the argument that (in the words of one of the latter's most energetic proselytizers) the "most important changes which have taken place in modern America have centered about a shift from small-scale, informal, locally or regionally oriented groups to large-scale, national, formal organizations . . . characterized by a bureaucratic structure of authority."

The second assumption behind Lippmann's argument was prescriptive: the wise course, even the moral course, for a society in the throes of such a transformation was not to resist these irresistible changes but to embrace them and attempt to control them—largely, although not exclusively, through government. The progressive/liberal project as it proceeded through the half century after Lippmann wrote displayed a great deal more ambivalence toward the idea of mastery than he believed it should. But the belief in both the inevitability and desirability of increasingly centralized power in modern societies has been a powerful strain within liberalism, and within the government dominated by liberalism, for generations—through the age of progressive reforms in the first years of the century, through the New Deal, through the Great Society, and (albeit in much diminished form) into our own time.

What can we say today about the assumptions behind the dream of "mastery"? Not that they are entirely wrong. The growth of large-scale organizations and the emergence of powerful nationalizing (and now internationalizing) forces in modern society—Lippmann's description of the character of the industrial world—are surely among the most important phenomena of the twentieth century. The nation and the world have become steadily more centralized, consolidated, bureaucratized in the eight decades since Lippmann wrote. There are few signs that this process is abating.

And what of Lippmann's second assumption, his prescriptive belief in the importance of "mastery," of introducing rational plan "to the jungles of disordered growth."
That remains a goal of almost everyone who works within large organizations, whether they be public or private. It
is a goal that, in limited ways at least, Americans have
sometimes achieved. There are economies of scale in the
modern polity; there are efficiently run bureaucracies that
serve as effective agents of growth and progress; there are
ways in which government planning and direction have
been and remain indispensable to the effective functioning
of our modern, integrated economy. The belief in "mastery," and even the reality of "mastery" in some realms,
still survives.

And yet if the assumptions Lippmann expressed have
not vanished from our world, neither are they wholly con-
vincing. As a description of modern society, the organizational ideal is clearly incomplete. For all the very real
centralization in the United States in this century, modern
America is still at least as notable for the degree to which it
has remained decentralized, for the extent to which the
United States has not forged a truly national society, for the
way in which localism, regionalism, ethnic and racial and
religious parochialism have survived and even flourished.
Even in terms of the economy, which defenders of the organizational ideal have always cited as the real proof of their
claims, the large-scale organization—important as it is—is
not the setting within which most people work or live. Small
businesses remain the largest sector of our economy, and
the number of independent workers, professionals, and
entrepreneurs has been steadily growing in both absolute
and relative terms. American government, for all its
undoubted expansion, remains in many ways the same frag-
mented and decentralized set of institutions that the framers

of our federal system envisioned. Except in a few areas, moreover, it is largely reactive—responding to entreaties and pressures from without and only rarely implementing coherent plans of its own.

As a prescription for modern society—an invocation to embrace the idea of mastery and centralized control as the principal moral project of our time—the organizational ideal seems now almost wholly to have lost the confidence of the nation. It was never dominant, never uncontested even in what seemed to be its most triumphant moments. It is now largely without defenders. For in our time, nothing seems to produce more contempt than the idea that there are solutions to our problems in the ideas of experts and the workings of bureaucracies. Very few people any longer believe that large organizations—least of all large governmental organizations—are capable of doing very much at all.

What has happened to destroy the faith that Lippmann expressed in 1915 and that survived, with varying degrees of strength, for many decades? The most important explanation is that there have been vast changes in the nation and the world that have created new and difficult problems. Americans have expected governments to solve those problems, and governments have not done so:

◆   The national and world economies have been changed profoundly and jarringly, in ways that have disoriented our society. The pressures of globalization have contributed to the phenomena of corporate "downsizing" and the significant increase in income inequality that have become central problems of our time. Globalization has not only created these problems. It has also made it far more difficult for governments to solve them, or indeed to shape the economic lives of their nations in any substantial way.

◆   In part as a result of these broad economic changes, a
corrosive fiscal crisis has undermined the ability of the federal government to perform. Budget deficits have ballooned;
the national debt has grown exponentially, adding to the
strains on the budget; entitlement costs have spiraled (and
will soon increase even more dramatically as the large population cohort born after World War II ages). The fiscal crisis has placed powerful constraints on the government's
ability to confront even the most urgent of our problems.
Perhaps equally seriously, it has undermined public faith in
its ability to behave responsibly. Whatever one thinks of
the economic consequences of the deficit, its political effects
have been incalculable.

◆   The nation's population and culture have been characterized by unprecedented diversity in the past several decades.
That is the result in part of new waves of immigration—
the largest since the late nineteenth century—but it is at
least as much the result of the destruction of many of the
barriers that once excluded some groups from the center of
national life. America has always been a diverse society, but
through most of its history it has contained the effects of
diversity within a series of rigid and often oppressive social
and political structures. Now that those structures are col-
lapsing, diversity has become inescapable—and at times
painful. It has placed great strains on our culture, on our
educational system, and on our faith in the ability of our
society to cohere.

◆   The international system that shaped American foreign
relations for nearly fifty years has now collapsed. And while
few lament the end of the cold war, many have found the
new and far less coherent patterns of international relations
of the 1990s confusing and frightening. Certainly, the federal

government—the presidency in particular—has suffered from
the loss of urgency and legitimacy that the cold war provided.

◆   Finally, there has been a broad shift in American culture, stretching now across more than forty years, that has
emphasized individual freedom, consumption, and personal
fulfillment over older notions of discipline, restraint, repres-
sion, and duty to the community. There has been, as many
have noted, an erosion in traditional patterns of civic life, a
fracturing of many of the social bonds that make it possible
for both local and national communities to flourish.
Traditional patterns of authority have frayed. Fewer Americans have an instinctive respect for public institutions; many
more have come to believe that, in our time, every individual
is largely on his or her own. There is much to be said for this
new culture and for the liberation from artificial restraints it
has encouraged. But it has also created an environment in
which government and many other institutions have much
more difficulty winning popular respect.

Government has not been the cause, at least not the principal cause, of any of those changes. But neither has it been
able to manage the problems they have produced to the satis-
faction of the public. The result is our present political
moment—in which leaders of both parties vie with one another in expressing their hostility to big government, in pro-
claiming their faith in local and private solutions to what used
to be considered national and public problems, and in proposing measures to free the entrepreneurial talents of the nation
from the shackles of centralized regulation and control.

✳   ✳   ✳

Government may not be responsible for most of the vast
social and economic changes it has tried unsuccessfully to

control. But it has responded to those changes (and to its own failure to master them) in ways that have contributed significantly to the public's loss of faith in politics and bureaucracy. There is a debilitating internal dynamic at work in public life. It has emerged directly out of the popular resentment government increasingly attracts, and out of the efforts of public officials to protect themselves against that resentment.

Those who work in government are acutely conscious of the changed climate in which they now perform. They are aware of the heightened scrutiny they are likely to receive, of the passion for scandal that drives much of the media, of the intolerance for failure among members of the public. They realize that in the increasingly adversarial politics of our time they are vulnerable at any moment to investigations, hearings, public denunciations, even criminal prosecutions for behavior that in the past attracted little or no notice outside the bureaucracies themselves. And so they respond in increasingly defensive ways that are both understandable and self-destructive, ways that in fact worsen the problems they are designed to avoid.

Several related concerns in particular seem to have emerged out of the relentless popular attacks on government, all of which make bureaucracies more alienating and less responsive than they would otherwise be. The most powerful, perhaps, is the fear of scandal, which leads to the creation of increasingly elaborate rules and procedures that are stultifying to public service and alienating to those citizens who must deal with government agencies. Another is the fear of failure—the belief that any public effort that does not succeed will destroy the reputations and perhaps the careers of those who undertake them; the result is a widespread reluctance to experiment, a fear of innovation, a desperate clinging to safe, uncontroversial ways even if they are ineffective or counterproductive. A third is the fear of discretionary authority, a reluctance to permit lower-level officials to make any significant decisions on their own (lest they create scandal or failure), leading to a top-heavy decisionmaking process characterized by inefficiency, delay, and bureaucratic stagnation.

All such processes have been visible in large bureaucracies for as long as they have existed. But with government agencies and public officials feeling the weight of popular opprobrium, they have become more powerful and more debilitating than at any time in recent memory. The more unpopular government becomes, the more public officials seek to defend themselves against accusations of impropriety or incompetence. And the more bureaucracies try to defend themselves, the worse their performance usually gets.

Similar dynamics affect the way elected officials behave. Aware of the contempt with which the public views their calling, they become morbidly sensitive to swings in public opinion. Fearful that voters will not trust anything they say, they tailor their rhetoric to what they believe are prevailing popular views—whether or not those views accord with reality. Nothing is more central to the antigovernment ethos of our time than the widespread belief that politicians seldom tell the truth. While that belief is undoubtedly exaggerated, it is certainly the case that many politicians measure what they know to be the truth against what they fear to be the likely popular response to it; in such contests, the truth is often overmatched. This pattern, too, has been characteristic of politics since time immemorial. But in an age of antigovernment fervor, the pattern has spread, poisoning the relationship between citizens and their representatives in countless ways. Politicians, like bureaucrats, seek to defend themselves from the public's wrath. In mounting that defense, they increase the anger.

It is not difficult, then, to understand why so many Americans have lost faith in government. And it is not difficult to conclude that, for those who believe in the positive uses of government, the major challenge of our time is finding a way to restore that eroded faith. But there are few obvious ways of doing that. The problems facing government are complicated and enormously difficult. Solutions, if solutions there are, will have to emerge from slow and patient efforts, and from a willingness to experiment and to tolerate failure. But any search for answers will be impossible in the absence of at least some minimal public trust in government. The quest for more effective public policies must be accompanied, therefore, by efforts to refurbish the reputation of public policy itself, and of the men and women who shape and implement it. Several broad initiatives might contribute to that task.

◆   One of the problems government now encounters in gaining public trust is matching its own everyday performance to the standards most of the public has come to expect from institutions in the private sector. Some government bureaucracies function quite well, of course. But many do not—unsurprisingly, since the frenzy of deficit reduction in the last two decades has left public agencies with greatly diminished budgets and far fewer personnel. Like all victims of downsizing, public bureaucracies have experienced both demoralization and a real reduction in their ability to perform their jobs effectively. So the widespread assumption that any encounter with a public agency will produce delay, inaction, and frustration is not an unreasonable one. One important goal of public life, therefore, is to enhance both the status and performance of public employees—by giving them the resources they need to do their jobs and by finding some way to elevate the calling of public service in our culture to a level that will enable it to attract more men and women of talent and commitment. In France, and in some other nations, being a member of the civil service is a position of real distinction, a career to which many of the nation's most talented and ambitious people aspire, a calling enhanced by the existence of a prestigious national academy of public service equivalent to their (and our) military academies. In the United States, civil servants have no such standing and the profession of public service no such prestige. If we hope to have a government worthy of popular trust and respect, we should find ways to help those who serve it win the same.

◆ The role of government in American life has a long history, some of it squalid, brutal, and destructive, but some of it efficient, effective, even visionary. Government programs have contributed to the development of the vast interior spaces of the nation in countless ways, to the discovery of new technologies, to the creation of distinguished educational systems, to the decline in poverty and disease in this century, to the increased security and prosperity of the elderly, and to countless other things. The story of American government's important and enduring achievements is familiar enough to those with a reasonable knowledge of our past; yet it is all but invisible in public discourse today and thus largely inaccessible to those whose knowledge of history is frail. It is surely an important task for defenders of the public sector to remind the public of the many things government has done, and continues to do, well, and of what would likely happen to the character and quality of our society should it cease to play a significant role.

◆ At the same time, defenders of government must avoid being uncritical of the institutions they have inherited. If it is important to make clear what government has done well, it is equally important to make clear the tasks at which government has failed, to point out what is wrong with existing policies and institutions. Advocates must make a clear case for what government can and should do in our time and must not fall back upon reflexive defenses of things as they are.

♦   Among the many causes of the growing disconnection between people and politics have been the changes in the style and character of popular politics in this century, and in particular in the past several decades. Politics has moved out of any significant place in the lives of communities and families and individuals, and into consulting firms, advertising offices, and television studios. One result is that the parties themselves play an increasingly attenuated role in public life. Another is that it is now far more difficult for individual voters to feel any real ties to the candidates and campaigns they are asked to support. Instead, politics has become an almost entirely passive activity that most voters encounter rarely and glancingly. They read capsule descriptions of campaigns in newspapers and magazines. They listen to the radio. Above all, they watch television. Occasionally, in dwindling numbers, they go to the polls and vote. For most people, apparently, that is not enough to make politics seem significant. Replicating the sense of engagement and empowerment that characterized earlier eras of party politics would be a difficult, perhaps even impossible, task, given the erosion of party structures and the overwhelming power of television in our world. But involving citizens in public life need not be restricted to campaigns, as the impressive growth of grass-roots political movements in recent years demonstrates. Leaders who wish to create some real sense of connection with their followers would do well to recognize that thousands of Americans have found a sense of engagement in working for specific, sometimes local, causes—environmentalism, education, feminism, antifeminism, and many others. Politicians would do well to look for ways to make these grassroots movements participants in the work of government.

◆   Finally, and most difficult of all, is another, equally important task awaiting those who hope to relegitimize political life in America. That is the task of introducing into political discourse habits of reasoned reflection, making it an activity we can take seriously as an intellectual endeavor. This is more complicated, and much more difficult, than the frequent demand by voters that our leaders tell the truth, although without a respect for truth political language will remain as empty and disrespected as it is now. It is the goal of making public leadership a search not just for power but also for knowledge. In recent years especially our politics has often seemed to be precisely the opposite, a flight from knowledge. The cultivation of ignorance—ignorance of the real nature of our problems, of the predictable consequences of our actions—has become a deliberate political style. It is little wonder that contempt for political language and political life has risen significantly in the past decade or so and that leaders at all levels now find it much more difficult to enlist even modest public confidence.

The search for knowledge is crucial precisely because we live in a time of such bewildering changes and corrosive cultural conflicts, which are all the more frightening because of our limited understanding of them. Historians writing of the late nineteenth and early twentieth centuries have noted, looking back on the anguished political rhetoric of those years, how imperfectly contemporaries understood the great social and economic forces that were the most important sources of their problems, how often they focused their anger and fear on things that were marginal to their plights or irrelevant altogether. Future historians of our own time will undoubtedly say the same of us: that we flailed away at ephemera and phantoms without understanding that our real task was to comprehend a series of profound structural changes in our society and our world.

But there were people in that earlier period of political crisis who believed that Americans could find a way genuinely to understand their dilemmas, and that effective political leadership could help them do so. One of them was Walter Lippmann, whose dream of mastery represented not just a faith in the need for government but a belief in the power of knowledge and truth in the conduct of public business.

Americans in Lippmann's time never did, and of course never could, achieve real mastery over the great historical forces that were shaping their world. But their effort to do so was responsible for some of the notable public achievements of the early twentieth century. In our own time, in a world considerably more complicated and more dangerous than the one Lippmann described, it would be foolish to assume we could do much better. Yet we too can try, as Lippmann put it, to "cultivate reflection," to attempt to understand and, when possible, "master" the forces that buffet us and bring such uncertainty and insecurity into our lives.

The government of a democracy can do only so much; and one of the tasks of modern leadership is to help citizens understand the limits of government's capacities. But government can do something. Leading us in an effort to comprehend our world, and what we can and cannot do to control it, would be a good place for those who hope to refurbish the tattered reputation of American public life to begin.

Part
5

The Next Millennium

Chapter

17

THE PRIVATIZATION OF PUBLIC DISCOURSE

by Alan Brinkley

T he sudden rise of new vehicles of communication—and the possibility that they may transform the way in which Americans conduct their politics—raises a major question for public life. What kind of public discourse is necessary to sustain a healthy deliberative democracy? At one level, the answers are relatively simple.

First, it must be broadly accessible. Citizens must feel that they have a voice in the process by which decisions affecting their lives are made. They must believe that the means of deliberation that produce those decisions are fair—and that they are open, on a reasonably equal basis, to everyone.

Second, it must be at least minimally consensual. Citizens must have enough respect for the processes of decisionmaking, and enough faith in their fairness, to be willing to accept their results, even when the results are not to their liking.

The links between these two requirements are obvious. Without faith in the essentially democratic character of the process, respect for the system vanishes; its legitimacy weakens. Without respect for the system (and acceptance of its results), democratic procedures are, in the end, pointless since they can produce no real decisions.

Not many Americans today appear to believe that our public world meets either of those criteria. Complaints about the character of public discourse are many and various. They include the charge that ordinary people have no real access to the civic conversation, that the power to deliberate is contained within small groups of elites. But they also include the complaint that public discourse has, in a sense, become too open, too uninhibited; it has become unhappily freed from the healthy restraint, the respect for convention, that permits debate to remain civil and constructive. To some, public discourse is the smug murmur of people in power, who take no notice of the larger world. To others, it is the cacophony of coarse, harsh voices intent on vilifying individuals and institutions and promoting narrow, selfish, and often bizarre demands. And to many more, perhaps most dismayingly, it is both: a closed world of influence, with a crass and at times ugly clamor at the gates.

Is there anything new in these discontents? After all, complaints about the character of public discourse have been a staple of American political rhetoric since well before the American Revolution. There have always been critics who have denounced the degree to which elites dominate political debate and decisionmaking. And there have always been those who decry what they consider the coarseness and vulgarity of popular discourse. But to say that there are precedents for our current dissatisfaction is not to deny

that there is anything new. For there is something different
about the form of public conversation in our time—different from earlier times and certainly different from any ideal
vision of the character of democratic deliberation. That difference can be described most simply as the privatization
of public discourse.

*   *   *

This privatization is perhaps most evident in the disappearance of public forums for participation in civic discourse. Their disappearance has been long in the making,
but it has been exceptionally noticeable, and the effects have
become especially corrosive, in the relatively recent past.
There has, in fact, been a fundamental change in the character of our political life in recent decades, and that change
has left many citizens with a strong sense of their power-
lessness within and irrelevance to the process.

Politics in America was once very different from its present, embittered state. Throughout much of the nineteenth
century, and even part of the twentieth, politics was not for
most Americans a remote process to be shunned and reviled
but a vibrant, public activity that engaged the loyalty, even
the zeal, of millions of people. The eligible electorate was, to
be sure, severely restricted until well into the twentieth century. African-Americans, Indians, and other minorities could
vote almost nowhere in the nineteenth century. Women were
denied the franchise until a few states began permitting
them to vote shortly before the century's end. In some
states—most notably in the South—many poor whites were
effectively disenfranchised as well. But for those who did vote
(which in most of the nation was the vast majority of white
men), politics was often something close to a passion—
a passion kept alive by its intensely public character.

Campaigns centered around rallies, parades, barbecues, speeches, and lectures. Parties served social and cultural as well as political functions and played a major role in communities. They mobilized families, neighborhoods, even entire regions behind a set of public symbols and shared values. Seventy percent or more of the eligible electorate voted in every presidential election from 1840 to 1900; at times, the number rose above 80 percent. Even congressional elections routinely attracted 60 or 70 percent of the vote.

During the first half of the twentieth century—even though party loyalty and voter participation were declining—politics retained a considerable degree of vibrancy. Many local party organizations continued to thrive; participation in campaigns by volunteers remained high; grassroots political activity was still a significant part of the lives of many communities. As late as the mid-1960s, thousands, perhaps millions, of Americans developed a sense of engagement with the political system through broad-based, grassroots activity on behalf of John and Robert Kennedy, Lyndon Johnson, Barry Goldwater, Eugene McCarthy, George Wallace, and others.

There is, of course, much to criticize in this older political ethos: the restriction of the franchise, the shallowness of much political discourse, the hidden (and often not so hidden) power of bosses and machines that the public activities of parties and campaigns often served to disguise. One could argue that, in terms of policy results, American government for many years performed better—more creatively, more productively, more honestly—after the decline of mass-based party politics than it did in the heyday of parties. Even so, it would be hard to argue that politics today—whatever progress it has made in freeing itself from older obstacles and injustices—has managed to sustain the respect or legitimacy many Americans once accorded it. And it is clear, too, that this erosion of respect is now threatening the ability of government to craft good policy as well.

Politics has become remote from the lives of most Americans today in part because the intensely public activities that were once so central to civic life have come to seem part of a vanished world. That ordinary citizens were really involved in public conversation, actually a part of the decisionmaking process, may have been an illusion in the nineteenth and early twentieth century; but for those with access to the franchise, at least, it was a valuable illusion, and it made political activity lively and, for most voters, rewarding. In our own time, it is rarely possible for voters to sustain even the illusion of real participation in political life. Grassroots activity survives in America today and in many places flourishes. But seldom is it tied to the process by which we claim to keep alive the meaning of deliberative democracy: electoral politics. Environmentalists, right-to-life supporters, defenders of choice, multiculturalists, and many others mobilize communities actively and enthusiastically; sometimes they intervene in campaigns to exert pressure on behalf of their chosen issues. But parties and electoral politics mobilize no such popular enthusiasm or support. Campaigns are no longer part of the streets and the neighborhoods, the union halls and the local party headquarters. In most places, they have moved into television studios, advertising firms, and the offices of consultants and pollsters.

One recent, partial exception perhaps proves the rule: the first months of the 1992 campaign of Ross Perot. In the early stages of that campaign, before Perot's precipitous and temporary withdrawal from the race, it produced something that had long been missing from American politics, and partly as a result it enjoyed astonishing success. For it gave millions of voters the chance to feel that they were part of a genuine popular movement. The enthusiasm of those citizens was not just for, probably not even mainly for, Perot himself, about whom most people then knew very little (and who subsequently showed himself to be relatively unsympathetic to the exuberantly democratic grassroots politics he briefly and inadvertently helped produce). It was an enthusiasm for the idea of political participation: for collecting signatures, organizing local campaign committees, passing out buttons and bumper stickers. For a short time, some Perot supporters experienced a small dose of the sense of empowerment that made the civil rights movement, the antiwar protests, the New Left, and the right-to-life movement so alluring in the United States. Perot made it possible for his supporters to feel (however briefly and artificially) that they were controlling the process and not being controlled by it.

Much has been written in recent years about the death of civic life in America, about the difficulty citizens have in feeling connected to one another or in forming associations that give them a genuine sense of community. Such critiques are not uncontested. But even those who argue for the continued vibrancy of American civic life do not use politics to support their cause. When Americans engage in public activity today, they very rarely engage in politics. To many, in fact, politics has come to seem the antithesis of civic life—a harsh, closed world, a world in which nothing is real and nothing is true. And while there are many explanations for this alienation, it is hard to believe that the death of healthy public forums for political activity is not one of the most important.

*   *   *

At the same time that public forums for democratic discourse have declined, a new species of private ones has emerged in their place—forums that give the illusion but not the reality of genuine public conversation. The most powerful of these, of course, is television, which has been dominating and reshaping our politics now for two generations. No force is more responsible for taking politics out of the hands of parties and voters. None has done more to create the sense of alienation from the public sphere that now characterizes our national life.

In the last several years, however, another, newer medium of communication has become the subject of intense public interest and has inspired some hopes for a revival of genuine deliberative discussion: the Internet. The Internet provides something that more conventional public life has ceased to offer: a voice, a way for individuals to project their views into the world. But for the most part, it does so in ways that contribute relatively little to the kind of healthy public discourse a democratic society should hope to sustain; indeed, it often does so in ways that are in some respects hostile to that kind of discourse. Many of the voices heard in this new media are not part of a deliberative process, or even a part of a conversation. They are the voices of people speaking alone.

The Internet is not, certainly, a malign force in American life. On the contrary, it opens up breathtaking possibilities for new kinds of communication and broader access to information. It creates "virtual communities" among men and women of similar interests. At times, it produces sustained, intelligent conversation among far-flung people who would otherwise have no real contact with one another at all. It is certainly here to stay, and it is clearly becoming not only useful but invaluable to many areas of modern life.

But one purpose the Internet shows no signs of being able to serve effectively is advancing popular deliberation and decisionmaking. The kind of public exchanges that the new electronic media sometimes produce often seem, in fact, antithetical to decisionmaking. They appear to invite, instead, a kind of harsh, uncompromising dogmatism that competes with, and sometimes overpowers, rational dialogue. And the reason for that, one might speculate, is the essential privacy involved in the act of communicating through these vehicles.

These newer forms of communication are unmediated by the social conventions of restraint and accommodation that often (although certainly not always) shape public contact among people. Instead, they have produced conventions of their own: a new kind of abrupt, direct, and often confrontational form of discourse, in which ordinary forms of courtesy and deference (even if feigned) are not only absent but also often scorned.

The sociologists Lee Sproull and Sara Kiesler did a series of psychological experiments and organizational studies several years ago about the effects of electronic communication on large bureaucracies. They compared groups who met face to face with other groups working on similar problems but communicating with one another via electronic mail. Sproull and Kiesler discovered that within the groups communicating by e-mail, employees (particularly lower-ranking ones) were more likely to speak up, more likely to take initiative in proposing courses of action. On one level, in other words, electronic communication was unusually democratic. But Sproull and Kiesler also discovered that members of the e-mail groups were much more likely to express hostility and much less likely to compromise their views; thus they had greater difficulty reaching consensus. Emboldened to speak by the privacy of the medium, such men and women are isolated from the social settings that might otherwise foster the kind of dialogue capable of producing agreement.

They are also unaffected by the kind of temporal delay that in other media often leads to reflection and reconsideration and screens out particularly rash and abusive statements. The Harry S Truman Library contains many abrupt, furious, confrontational letters that President Truman wrote in fits of pique—letters that, had he actually sent them, would almost certainly have poisoned his relationships with any number of public and private figures. But Truman almost never mailed such letters. He wrote them late at night, put them in a drawer, and thought better of it the next day. Had he been working on e-mail, these angry missives might have been delivered in a keystroke—leaving the president, and the polity, to deal with the unhappy consequences. The presidency of Richard Nixon was notable for, among many other things, the intemperate—at times almost crazy—directives that Nixon ordered his aides to deliver to subordinates; H. R. Haldeman, John Ehrlichman, and others considered it part of their jobs to take no action on such orders and to give the president time to reconsider. In a world of instantaneous communication, a world in which Nixon's wildest ideas could be transmitted through the government with the touch of a button, the consequences of his festering, late-night resentments might well have been even more disastrous than they actually were.

The Internet does not, of course, create the angry and confrontational sentiments it often conveys. Such sentiments are a normal part of everyone's emotional arsenal. But the Internet does encourage what would otherwise often be unspoken thoughts to become highly public. And that is because for most people, communicating through the Internet is an intensely private experience. People writing on the Internet almost always do so alone; sometimes they do so anonymously. They have no need to consider the awkward, chastening consequences that would result from speaking abruptly or harshly in a public setting, or even in the more formal and ritualized world of written communication.

Angry and confrontational discourse, even coarse and vulgar discourse, are not always bad—whether on the Internet, on talk radio, or elsewhere. Jarring and even offensive communication often serves a valuable social purpose. It can unsettle unjustly settled conventions. It can challenge and even shake corrupt or illegitimate power. But a healthy democracy needs to be able to balance this kind of talk against another kind. It needs to create settings in which citizens can communicate with, and challenge, one another openly—settings in which some rules and conventions apply and where eventual accommodation and agreement is at least possible. The rise of these newer, more abrasive forms of verbal exchange is in part simply a result of new technologies and new customs. But it is also, I suspect, a result of the way many frustrated citizens of our society yearn for a voice, a way to make themselves heard. The public world, the political arena, offers them no such voice. They have turned to this alternative, quasi-private world instead.

From time to time in recent years, journalists, scholars, and even a few politicians have talked optimistically about the democratic potential of new forms of communication. Everyone will be linked to the information highway, and the nation's leaders, rather than allowing themselves to be buffeted by the conflicting pressures of special interests and imperfect reflections of public opinion, will be able to open the decisionmaking process to the public. A controversial measure could be subjected to a virtually instant referendum by allowing people to vote over the Internet. The electorate could function as a constant, direct force in policymaking. Leaders could truly represent the will of their constituents.

But it does not take much imagination to envision the possible consequences of this kind of direct democracy. Suppose the American people had been polled in the first hours after the Oklahoma City bombing about deporting Arab-Americans, who were initially (and falsely) assumed to be responsible? Suppose in Israel there were a referendum on how to deal with Arabs in the aftermath of a terrorist bombing? Suppose in the full frenzy of McCarthyism there had been a referendum on whether basic civil liberties should be protected? Would any of us feel confident that the results of such a process—a process of instantaneous, perhaps visceral, decisionmaking by individuals acting in solitude—would be what the electorate would welcome a decade, a year, even a week after the voting? Would we predict equally disheartening results in such circumstances from a sustained, public, deliberative process, in which passion and prejudice might be countered with reasoned argument?

Even now, the feature of our politics that many Americans seem most to dislike is the slavish attention of politicians to the polls, the mail, the telephone calls—in short, to the unending and at times radical fluctuations in public opinion. We claim to want politicians to pay attention to us, but we seem not to like it when they do—or at least when they do it too ardently and obviously. The closer Americans come to direct democracy, the less we seem to admire or respect our leaders and their politics.

Representative democracy, deliberative democracy, should not mean a democracy in which leaders pay no attention to the voters between elections. It should mean a politics in which all citizens have some chance to be heard and some sense of connection with the decisionmaking process. It should make possible forums in which loud, confrontational, abrasive, even vulgar voices can be a part of the public conversation. But it should also be a system in

which citizens have ample opportunity not just to speak—
not just to vent their unmediated feelings in private
settings—but to engage as well in open discourse with
others. Citizens of a democracy need to be heard. They
also need to listen. And they need to be able to do both in
public settings, where the search for agreement is at least
as highly valued as the need for individual expression.

Chapter

18

THE ROLE OF THE MEDIA IN REPRESENTATIVE GOVERNMENT

by Kathleen M. Sullivan

C riticism of the press's role in government lately has been sharp but contradictory. On the one hand, the press is attacked for having too big an effect on democratic deliberations. By ferreting out political or personal scandals, say the critics, the press drives good people away from politics. By choosing sensational news coverage to boost ratings, the press distorts the agenda for public policy-making. If the local nightly news dwells on brutal and graphic crime stories, politicians are forced to call for tough-on-crime measures even if the crime rate is dropping and the measures make bad crime policy. By covering political contests as horse races, critics assert, the press diverts attention from complex and serious policy issues. Voters learn more about what is at stake for politicians in an election than about what is at stake for them. The print media,

faced with competition from twenty-four-hour news services, increasingly publishes biased analysis in place of
facts. And the electronic media, by reducing political issues
to sound bites of ten seconds or less, encourage political figures to engage in shrillness and mutual vilification rather
than informed and dispassionate debate. On this view, the
press is a powerful actor whose effects on politics have
been largely negative.

On the other hand, the press is criticized equally harshly for weakness—for being too supine in the face of government. On this view, the press corps prizes access to
politicians and their staffs so highly that it pulls its punch-
es to avoid offending them. It is cowed by the government's
own elaborate spin-control machinery, giving in to pressure
to withhold unflattering stories. It is reactive in its coverage
of political campaigns, trailing around obediently to cover
carefully scripted appearances and raising tough issues
about a candidate only when the candidate's opponent does.
It is "scandal-shy," shirking exposure of sexual or financial wrongdoing that might harm politically powerful players, or might cause the public to disparage it as predatory.
On this view, the institution that ought to serve as the
watchdog of government has become a lapdog.

What should government do about these criticisms of
the press? Absolutely nothing—at least absolutely nothing
that aims at the content of media coverage of politics. That
is because the press enjoys strong First Amendment protection for good reason. Some have likened the press to a fourth
branch of government, providing the ultimate check and
balance that prevents tyranny by the other three. The institutional press can monitor government more closely than
individuals can, exposing public officials' errors and abuses
to public criticism and making room for political dissent.
A free press can also improve the quality of democratic

decisionmaking. It disseminates not only facts but also ideas from diverse and mutually antagonistic sources. By enabling a variety of viewpoints to be aired on controversial public matters, it can inform and alter the making of public policy.

For these reasons, the Supreme Court has repeatedly held that press freedom should be "uninhibited, robust and wide-open," in Justice William Brennan's words. The Court has invalidated licensing schemes, prior restraints, gag orders, and special taxes imposed upon the press. It has held that public officials have to endure even "vehement, caustic, and sometimes unpleasantly sharp attacks" upon them unless the press deliberately or recklessly prints false-hoods. It has given the press substantial access rights to tri-als and other official proceedings, preventing government from operating in ways that are secretive or corrupt. In short, it has given the press substantial immunity from gov-ernment restraint or retaliation.

What if the government tries to improve rather than censor the content of press coverage? Some contemporary press critics, for example, suggest that broadcasters and cable operators should be required to provide more or bet-ter public affairs programming, or free airtime for the expression of candidates' views. Others suggest that third party and independent candidates ought to be guaranteed more access to political coverage and televised debates. The government's few prior ventures into fine-tuning the content of the electronic media illustrate that this approach is seri-ously misguided. For some years the Federal Communi-cations Commission required broadcasters to give free time for response to personal attacks or controversial political editorials. This so-called fairness doctrine could never have been imposed on the print media, which have broad edito-rial discretion as a matter of constitutional right. But the FCC viewed broadcast stations as a scarcer resource than

printing presses and so held, with the Supreme Court's bless-
ing, that they could be conscripted as conduits for the
speech of others in order to maintain diversity of views.

The FCC has repealed the fairness doctrine, and
Congress has failed to resurrect it by legislation. The reason
is the death of scarcity; with more space on the electromag-
netic spectrum and with the growth of satellite technology
and cable, it could no longer be said that broadcasters held
any choke-hold monopoly. But the reason may as well have
been the failure of the fairness doctrine to serve its purposes: although rights of reply were meant to ensure vigorous
debate on controversial issues, they in fact tended to encourage reticence and blandness as stations strove to avoid controversial statements that would trigger right-of-reply
obligations. Forcing mainstream stations to carry a few,
token adversarial viewpoints proved far less effective in
increasing diversity of coverage than alternatives such as
subsidizing public radio and television.

Any solution to existing problems in press coverage
thus should come from the press itself rather than the government. There is much evidence that the press is responsive
to public criticism, even to a fault. For instance, prompted
by prominent public criticism of its sound-bite tendencies,
every major broadcast and cable network devoted some
amount of free airtime during the 1996 presidential campaign to lengthy, unedited statements by all the principal
candidates. For another more dubious example, many local
news outlets have experimented with "public journalism,"
which encourages ordinary citizens rather than journalists to
set the agenda of issues for public affairs coverage. This
movement seeks to emulate the success of talk radio and
"town hall" television debate formats. While there is considerable merit to expanding the range of subject matter
coverage, public journalists depart too far from valuable

professional norms and customs when they make journalism a matter of mere market testing. One of the assumptions on which robust First Amendment protection rests is that the press governs itself by ethical norms of impartiality, independence, fairness, and objectivity that make it beholden neither to government nor to special interest constituencies. Compromising this independence might undermine the arguments for freedom from government regulation.

Arguments for government regulation of media content should therefore be rejected. They violate basic First Amendment principles. They threaten the press's watchdog role. But they also entirely miss a key point: the most important problem with the media in our current politics is not content but structure. The print and electronic media have always been privately owned, and it has long been true, as A. J. Liebling quipped, that "freedom of the press is guaranteed only to those who own one." But, just at the moment when we are experiencing the greatest decentralization of information the world has ever known across the global web of linked computers known as the Internet, we are also seeing an unprecedented wave of corporate concentration in the media industry. NBC is owned by General Electric, and, in a rash of recent mergers, the Disney Company took over ABC, Westinghouse took over CBS, and Time Warner merged with Turner Broadcasting, the home of the twenty-four-hour news service CNN. The corporate alliance of the news industry with giants of entertainment and defense raises serious questions. Will those who produce the news within such corporate structures be willing to bite the hand that feeds them? To pan their movies or to cover corporate scandals? To question the safety of their products or the wisdom of their procurement of government funds? To cover their political contributions? To devote coverage to the phenomenon of media concentration in itself? Some networks have

already, in notorious incidents, pulled or apologized for negative coverage of the tobacco industry, in which their corporate owners held substantial financial interests. Of further
concern is the possibility that concentrated media ownership will make the information delivered to the public
increasingly centrist, homogeneous, and bland. Some radio
stations and commentators have already been dropped, post-
merger, because they were perceived as too far outside the
political mainstream.

The First Amendment poses far less an obstacle to government regulation of media structure than media content.
The free speech and press guarantees have never exempted
the press from the reach of content-neutral laws, including,
most relevantly, antitrust laws. The Supreme Court has held,
for example, that cable operators may be required to carry
local broadcast stations if their control over the cable con-
duit and their vertical integration with cable programmers
poses a competitive threat to the broadcast system. The
reason is that such a law aims at the economic structure of
the industry, not at any programming the systems carry. If a
television is, as one FCC commissioner once remarked, a
"toaster with pictures," the government is as free to regulate
the toaster as it is bound to leave the protected content of
the pictures alone.

Yet government has lately shied away from addressing
seriously the problems of media oligopoly and cross-
ownership posed by the recent wave of concentration. This
hands-off approach should be reexamined. Closer scrutiny
of deals under existing antitrust laws would be desirable.
The solution might be to separate conduits from content—
to require corporations to choose between making programs
and carrying them. Or the solution might be to tax the use
of the public broadcast spectrum and to direct the resulting
revenues toward expanding publicly subsidized radio and

television stations, so long as government leaves them edi-torial control. Of course, there are countervailing argu-ments: some say that large-scale media companies are needed to do battle in an increasingly global competition; others suggest that freedom of expression on the Internet undermines the ability of the corporate media to homoge-nize ideas or exert ideological domination, so that the prob-lem is self-limiting.

These questions are quite complex, but one thing about them is straightforward: the First Amendment does not place any gag order on asking them. Freedom of speech and press entails some limits on economic regulation; special taxation of the press, for example, has rightly been held to be cen-sorship by other means. But the First Amendment is mis-read when invoked as a bar to all regulation of media market structure. Government need not treat all the institutions of the press as if they were lone orators on soapboxes. The misguided focus on fine-tuning press content has diverted attention from this more important structural debate.

Chapter

19

CONSTITUTIONAL ANGST: DOES AMERICAN DEMOCRACY WORK?

by Nelson W. Polsby

I

It is only a small exaggeration to say that among the dubious benefits Americans have received from the collapse of the Soviet Union and its associated authoritarian regimes is an increase in the number and volume of voices saying that democracy in America does not work very well. Evidently an adversarial world order helps to forestall the more corrosive sorts of American self-appraisal. But the current global environment provides no credible military threats to American democracy. This has created what might be called a severe angst gap in the United States, a gap that anguished voices from all points in the political spectrum are working overtime to fill.

Former members of the cabinet and political advisers to presidents of the United States, for example, are on record urging fundamental constitutional reform so as to discourage stalemate in decisionmaking and to increase accountability of political leaders to voters. Conservative legislators are sponsoring a variety of constitutional amendments limiting the terms of office of members of Congress, establishing a line-item veto for presidents, and requiring balanced budgets. A new liberal journal of public affairs says in its manifesto:

> The health of democracy in America, after all, is not good. The relations of politics, money, and the media have deformed our traditions. Cynicism about politics is pervasive; "politician" and "bureaucrat" are terms of abuse. Voter turnout has fallen to a level that ought to be a national embarrassment. . . .

Referring to a "rigged political system," a liberal public interest lobbyist charges that "the current system of financing elections for the U.S. Congress is patently unfair." He says, "We are actually losing our ability to have real congressional elections."

In the wake of a protracted struggle over the size and shape of the U.S. budget a few years ago, several mainstream news magazines—*Newsweek*, *U.S. News and World Report*, *Business Week*—declared the American political system bankrupt and called for massive reforms.

These criticisms may in part be phrased as complaints about policy outcomes, but they are not merely about the shape of public policy. Presumably critics of the system on the right would disagree with critics on the left about what constitutes appropriate public policy. And yet both are dissatisfied. So if we are to take the severe views they express seriously, we must ask more basic questions about whether the American political system has in fact failed as an experiment in democracy.

If a political system can be shown to be undemocratic, this demonstration lends considerable credence to the arguments of critics who are unhappy with the policies that system may produce. That is to say, such policies can be regarded as illegitimate. Thus, it seems important to ask whether the political system in the United States meets elementary criteria generally thought to be essential to democracy.

II

It may be helpful in this connection to draw upon what many scholars will recognize as a classic formula describing "processes and institutions of large-scale, representative democracy of the type developed in the 20th Century" or, in Robert Dahl's language, a polyarchy, in order to see whether the United States may be considered an example. Polyarchies are held to be defined by seven institutional characteristics, which can be used as a baseline for gauging contemporary American governmental performance. These characteristics are:

(1) elected officials,

(2) inclusive suffrage,

(3) the right to run for office,

(4) free and fair elections,

(5) freedom of expression,

(6) alternative information,

(7) associational autonomy.

The first four characteristics have to do with elections, of which the United States has a great many.

ELECTED OFFICIALS. At the national level, virtually all major policymaking in the United States requires action by elected officials, and to a degree unmatched elsewhere unelected policymakers not only serve formally at the pleasure of elected officials but typically in practice last in office only as long as the elected officials who appointed them. This is not true of the unelected bureaucratic mandarins who dominate policymaking in most advanced democratic nations. Unlike many democratic nations, the United States also has a full complement of elected officials at an intermediate distance from ordinary citizens, at the state level, with a range of responsibilities that within their sphere (for example, police, road maintenance) more or less correspond to those of national officials. There is yet another, local, level, with in many cases a rather full array of elected officials as well, including elected school boards and trustees of public sector organizations having specialized functions, such as transportation, water supply, or waste management.

Presumably, the main point about having elected officials predominate in the making of public policy is that if the general trend of public policy is unsatisfactory, or if one or more incidents with respect to policy or other aspects of the conduct of public officials incur the disapproval of the general populace, then at the next election the officials in charge can be replaced. Behaviors consequent to the threat of replacement, and to the desire of officials to forestall replacement, as well as to the actual replacement of public officials from time to time, are all thought to provide the sort of significant links between followers and leaders that entitles a political system to be classed as democratic.

INCLUSIVE SUFFRAGE. The second criterion identifies more fully the population that elected officials need to take into account in maintaining a democratic leader-follower relationship. Such a relationship requires that the followers be permitted in large numbers to vote. Like many modern democracies, the United States was late in granting suffrage to women (1920). More scandalously, Americans descended from African slaves were, with the acquiescence of the legal systems of states in the southeastern quadrant of the nation, denied the vote for more than a century after the abolition of slavery. The reorientation of the legal system in the 1960s to secure the voting rights of African-Americans was a fundamental achievement. In addition, the age of voting eligibility for all citizens has since 1971 dropped from twenty-one to eighteen. The right to vote in the United States is now quite inclusive.

Voting does, however, rely for execution on a fair measure of voluntarism, in that most localities demand proof of residence as a prerequisite for voting and expect would-be voters to take the initiative to register to vote. This frequently poses some practical problems for the one-third of Americans who change their home addresses in every two-year interval. The extreme geographic mobility of Americans and the highly localized tradition of control over the mechanics of voting has therefore, among other possible factors, limited the actual turnout of Americans at the polls. Legal restrictions also deny the right to vote to some ex-felons and all noncitizen aliens, of whom the United States has more than most democratic nations, as well as those declared mentally incompetent.

In this manner, over the past century notable advances in the inclusiveness of the right to vote have been achieved by the American political system. In the case of the vote for eighteen-year-olds, the change came without real struggle. In the cases of women and African-Americans, considerable effort was needed to counter resistance. Contemporary Americans look back for the most part with incredulity that this should have been the case, since none of these expansions of the right to vote proved even remotely desta- bilizing over the medium run to the political system. Indeed, it is arguable that only the civil rights expansion of the vote even had much of an impact on the relative strength of American political parties. Over the short run, the introduction of sizable increments of African-Americans into the electorate merely strengthened the politically dom- inant New Deal coalition. Over a slightly longer run, this change in the character of the electorate no doubt con- tributed by way of backlash to the rise of the Republican party in the South and hence to the transformation of the South into a political entity somewhat more like the rest of the country. Other elements of demographic change and modernization also were pushing the South in the same direction, and so one must conclude that the influence in isolation of the expansion of the suffrage on political change over the past century has been modest.

THE RIGHT TO RUN FOR OFFICE. The right to run for most public offices is not greatly constrained by legal restric- tions, but there are important practical obstacles with respect to the more visible and powerful positions. There is no compact way to describe rules of entry for public office in the United States because there is such diversity both in the pathways and in the offices themselves. Each of the fifty states of the Union constitutes a separate legal system and political culture, required only by the U.S. Constitution to provide a "republican form of government." In some states there are large numbers of elective offices in each locality; in some there are few. Some states encourage the formation of political parties at the local level to manage nomination processes; in some states local parties are banished from the ballot, and aspirants to local office must self-sponsor or affiliate with local civic organizations or interest groups.

Because of the widespread use of primary elections as the vehicle of choice for the making of nominations at all levels, some form of advertising in order to reach voters is frequently required. Advertising means finding and spending money, especially when the potential electorate is very large—as, for example, in congressional districts (population around 600,000) or cities of any size. Thus, the scale of American politics and its reliance on popular voting act in lieu of party organization to ration access to public office.

Most successful candidates for elective office nevertheless first gain the nomination of the Democratic or Republican party. These parties are virtually everywhere, located respectively on the left and right sides of whatever the current ideological spectrum is, but the actual content of issues dividing the parties frequently varies greatly from state to state. Thus, what may appear to European observers to be a relatively narrow set of alternative, practical, political options in fact accommodates quite a lot of variety because of the importance nearly everywhere of local considerations. The localism of American political organization is also reflected in the lack of strict party discipline, except on rare occasions, in national and state, and even local, legislatures.

Additionally, candidates run and are elected to public office without party designation at local levels where party labels are forbidden; and an appreciable, but on the whole electorally unsuccessful, flock of minor parties also run candidates for various public offices, up to and including the presidency. Public funding, which provides a substantial fraction of the finance for major party presidential campaigns, is for practical purposes more or less denied to smaller parties, but small-party candidates for all offices are not required to forfeit an electoral deposit if they do badly at the polls.

Many thoughtful people believe that Americans are living in an era of weak political parties, and that the strengthening of parties ought therefore to be high on the agenda for public discussion. In some respects, these people have a point. But it is probably worth mentioning that the weakness of American political parties has been enormously exaggerated because of the tendency of political observers to focus on the presidential nominating process, where state-level parties are indeed weak and uninfluential and the news media and primary electorates are dominant. A look at the larger picture tells a somewhat different story.

The term "political party" stands for at least three somewhat different processes. In the first place, it refers to those organizations that nominate candidates for public offices, get out the vote, sponsor campaigns, and register new voters. Such organizations tend to have employees (more in election years, fewer in off years), volunteers, offices, and telephones. They are regulated by state laws and tend to vary quite a lot from state to state, locality to locality. One thinks of the squeaky-clean politics of the states of the upper Midwest in comparison, say, with Louisiana, where former governor Earl Long once said that when he died he hoped he would be buried in Plaquemines Parish so that he could remain active in politics. Parties as nominating organizations tend to draw their strength from the grass roots, where most of the political business of

America is done and where most of the public offices—for state assembly, city council, and so forth—are located.

Political parties are also symbolic entities, constructs that voters carry around in their heads that help structure public opinion and voting behavior. Most voting Americans consider themselves either Democrats or Republicans—and, as mentioned, the vast majority of American public officials are either Democratic or Republican. In recent years, some surveys have detected what has looked like a "de-alignment" of American voters, in which unprecedented numbers of respondents have identified themselves not as Democrats or Republicans but as independents. This trend has given comfort (or discomfort) to observers who believe that political parties are weakening in their power to command the allegiance of the electorate. A strong counterargument points out that what the data really show is that roughly two-thirds of survey respondents who call themselves "independent" voters are actually loyal party voters—some Democrats, some Republicans. They may call themselves independents for many reasons. Americans do not like to be taken for granted, and many individuals evidently enjoy thinking of themselves as free to choose in each election. Indeed, they are, but two-thirds of them regularly freely choose according to what V. O. Key once described as a "standing decision" to back one party or the other absent overwhelming incentives to change. What these "independent" survey respondents are doing is suppressing their report of this standing decision until the follow-up question about which way they habitually "lean." A reasonable conclusion from this way of looking at the evidence is that party loyalty still exerts a strong pull on the opinions and allegiances of most voters and citizens. There is not very much to be gained by thinking about strategies for strengthening parties among the electorate.

A third aspect of political parties is visible in legislative bodies: city councils, state assemblies, and Congress, where for purposes of organizing committees and staffing the chamber members caucus according to the party banner under which they were elected. At local levels and in one or two states, nonpartisan elections were established by law, mostly during the Progressive Era (1890–1920), expressly to inhibit the influence of political parties on legislative activity. This effort has met with only modest success: voters and members generally know who the Democrats are in the formally nonpartisan San Francisco City Council and who the Republicans are in the nonpartisan, unicameral legislature of Nebraska.

I do not know of a comprehensive survey that measures the actual extent to which parties currently structure politics and the organization and voting of the myriad legislative bodies with which American states and localities are blessed. An effort in that direction by David Mayhew as of 1960 concluded that there were wide variations in the presence of party from place to place. These variations, rooted in the history, economics, and demographic profiles of different places, are as good an illustration as I know of the diversity of American political cultures. That such diverse microsystems fly only two flags, Democratic and Republican, suggests something of the power of the national government. If the activities of the federal government were less important, there would be fewer incentives for Texas Democrats to unite with Vermont Democrats and New Jersey Democrats in search of a governing coalition in Congress.

As to Congress, where the record keeping is excellent, the story of party cohesion there is unequivocal. Owing principally to the emergence of the Republican party in the southern states, the capacity of party caucuses in Congress to outline policy alternatives and achieve party-line voting has not been higher in nearly a century. Parties in Congress are stronger today than at any time in living memory, now that the power of the "Dixiecrats" to split the Democratic caucus has greatly diminished.

National party organizations today are raising and disbursing sizable amounts of money, recruiting candidates, coordinating congressional votes, and structuring the political preferences of millions of American voters. Does this mean that there is nothing to the common perception that American parties are in decline? In one arena, that of presidential nominations, parties are in decline. This of course does not constitute an argument that they should be strengthened. Some observers believe that a presidential nominating process such as now exists, featuring self-starting candidates who must compete with other self-starters for the favor of successive primary electorates, with the whole show mediated by news organizations, is in some sense more democratic than any process in which political parties take a larger role.

The ground for this belief has always seemed to me shaky, resting as it does exclusively on the observation that more people "participate" in primary elections than in the alternative delegate-selecting schemes—principally caucuses of party faithful—that prevailed in many states before they were outlawed by the Democrats in the party reforms of 1969–70. The more "participants," the argument went, the more democracy.

A more fine-grained analysis might have asked two further questions: What was it that participants were actually able to do? Did this participation embed itself in the overall process so that primary electorates could be said to be more representative of the overall party electorate or national electorate and better able, therefore, to express the preferences of the great mass of voters than the smaller number of participants they supplanted?

As virtually everyone now agrees, it was on these latter two points that the new arrangements fell down, proving to be a severe disappointment. State party elites merely gave way to those elites best able to manipulate the primary process. Presidential elections became strangely anomalous in the American political system as the majority party, the Democrats, winners of most elections to state assemblies, governorships, House, and Senate, lost the presidency time and again.

Why? The most persuasive explanation for this anomaly is that the reforms compelled a presidential nominating process in which coalition building among party leaders was discouraged and factional mobilization—each candidate trying to survive each primary election by bringing his and only his voters to the polls—became the strategy of choice. In the endgame, therefore, the party with the most factions and the most disagreements, the Democrats, had the hardest job of putting the pieces together to fight a general election. Thus, strengthening the parties in the presidential nominating process really means strengthening state parties at the expense of candidates. It means making the Democrats more competitive in general elections. It means restoring coalition building as a prime goal for candidates.

What caused state parties to abandon the nominating process was overregulation by the national Democratic party. State party leaders were told that delegates would not be seated at the national convention unless the delegate selection process (and its outcomes) in the states met a long laundry list of conditions. This restricted the options of party leaders and caused them not only to resort to primary elections but also to insulate most other party business from the presidential race, so as to protect against an unpredictable influx of single-shot enthusiasts.

If regulation was the proximate cause of the departure of state parties from the delegate selection process, presumably deregulation would help in restoring their participation. Two notes of caution need to be sounded in this connection. First, it is naive to think that all state parties are as they were twenty years ago. So the best it is reasonable to hope for is that the restoration of incentives for state parties to control their delegations will increase the ties between presidential selection and other party organizational activities—candidate recruitment, voter mobilization, and so on. Some state party elites will prove to be so unrepresentative and hidebound as to be unable to help in building a winning presidential coalition. But others will come back into the system and will constitute a force for party cohesion. Results, in short, will vary.

Second, there may be a few regulations that the national parties will find it prudent to retain. Prohibition against racial exclusion in the delegate selection process is an obvious example. Perhaps, for historically obvious reasons, it is the only such example.

FREE AND FAIR ELECTIONS. With the advent of voting machines and the decline of strong, monopolistic local parties, corruption in the counting of votes and in the general administration of elections has in recent decades become a rarity. Thus, with respect to the four criteria of polyarchy pertaining to elections, American political institutions appear, with the reservations indicated, comfortably to qualify as free and fair. Indeed, over the past few decades on most dimensions the United States has made modest gains, and in the case of the suffrage of African-Americans, dramatic gains.

The three remaining criteria of polyarchy refer to freedoms of expression, information, and association, all

explicitly guaranteed by the First and Fourteenth amendments to the U.S. Constitution and consequently secured by
judicial review and by the prevalence in the United States of
a culture of adversary legalism. This culture facilitates
recourse to the courts as a means of vindicating the constitutional rights of individuals and of institutions specialized to the expression of political views.

FREEDOM OF EXPRESSION. Freedom of expression on the
whole operates over a broader band today than was true a
few decades ago, as illustrated by the wide, public avail-
ability of printed words that once would have been seized
by the postal service or shut down by local vice squads.
Sexual minorities now freely exercise their rights to express
themselves. In the political sphere voices of dissent are regularly heard, and in some cases widely publicized. Some
of these voices are extremely divisive, and some perform
acts, such as flag burning, public marching, and picketing,
that stretch the meaning of speech. Mostly, these acts have
received legal protection under the First Amendment freedom of speech rubric.

ALTERNATIVE INFORMATION. In general, the legal climate
governing journalistic practice in the United States—weak
libel laws, strong First Amendment to the Constitution—
encourages the printing or the broadcast of nearly any
information that may be in a journalist's possession. It is
hence arguable that an unusually wide range of information
characteristically becomes available to citizens about the
leaders upon whom and the policies upon which they must
pass judgment. This conclusion is hotly disputed by
observers who are inclined to the belief that a sort of
Gresham's law of information operates in which trivia drive
out information more relevant to the disposition of public

policy. In general, however, the pessimistic view of informational constraints on voter choice is more likely to focus on such issues of overload or irrelevancy than on successful concealment.

As recently as the presidency of John Kennedy, manipulation by concealment would have been the more pressing problem. Not everyone applauds the evident decline since then in respect for the privacy of public officials. The swift march in norms of journalistic disclosure over the past thirty years, along with ever-tightening rules of conduct for officials, now regularly takes a fearsome toll on the reputations of the more visible public officials.

Because so many decisions are placed in the hands of electorates, in long ballots filled not only with choices for lesser public officials but also, in many states, with initiatives and referendums, the informational needs of voters, even when they do not outrun supply, simply exhaust their patience and their willingness to pay attention. This condition, when it occurs, is the precursor of a serious pathology of direct democracy, namely, de facto public policymaking not by multitudes of informed voters but by highly manipulative elites who may control the wording—frequently confusing—of measures proffered to the electorate and may undertake effective but untruthful advertising campaigns. Presumably a palliative for these ills of direct democracy is representative democracy because representatives can devote time and intelligence, staff, and specialized knowledge to deliberation on measures that come before them, including those measures that would strain the cognitive capacities of more casual participants.

The cognitive and informational problems of direct democracy do plague American electorates from time to time, especially in a progressive, large state like California, where referendums are an entrenched method of policymaking.

Similar problems afflict proposals to limit the terms of legislators by initiative, an extremely popular measure everywhere and successfully enacted in those states—roughly
half of them—where initiatives are permitted by the state
constitution. Such proposals would cripple the capabilities
of legislatures by limiting the experience they can accumu-
late, thus creating new informational problems for democratic policymaking.

While political information is in many respects a free
good, with television sets in more than 90 percent of
homes, several cable channels devoted to nothing but news,
highly professionalized news coverage on the main networks, and daily newspapers also widely and cheaply available, given what a citizen needs to know to make all the
decisions that citizens must make, it still may not be
enough.

There is no doubt, however, that there is a lot of information out there and that there are alternative sources.
Journalistic practices rather than political regulation frequently lead to convergence of coverage and create central
tendencies in the content of the news media. These tendencies as often as not are hostile to incumbents, an infre-
quently examined bias of the news media, but they are not
something that reduces the desire of incumbents to remain
accountable to electorates.

ASSOCIATIONAL AUTONOMY. Opportunities to associate
unconstrained by the government seem to the naked eye to
be as rich and varied today as when Tocqueville remarked
on the profusion of voluntary associations in the America of
a century and a half ago. I know of no census of such organizations, but I observe that with respect to at least one
subset there has been a notable recent increase. This is the
subset of groups making headquarters in Washington for

the purpose of influencing the federal government. The news media attempt to keep track of such organizations, and their number seems to be growing. This suggests that the capacity of citizens, variously organized, to express their views to the government is at least being maintained.

Interest groups have more than one purpose. A function collateral to that of attempting to influence the government is the building of the sort of social capital that helps hold the polity together. Recently an interesting argument has been made that those sorts of voluntary organizations that nurture political skills and civic trust have suffered a notable decline in the United States over the past few decades. It is not an argument that has as yet been fully tested empirically. At least a few elements must still be sorted out: the extent to which the decline in voluntary organizational life mirrors the entry of women into the paid workforce, for example, might lead analysts to think of the time of citizens as having been traded off rather than wasted. Electronic and other sophisticated forms of communication responsive to voluntary manipulation may have liberated Americans from the geographic constraints of primary group interaction and therefore redistributed rather than obliterated associational life. There is a regular progression in the preferences of Americans that replaces batch processing of all sorts—trains, trolleys, apartments, bowling leagues—with lives that are more customized and independently controlled—cars, suburbs, bowling alone or in small groups. My own belief is that, even after these aspects of the argument are fully worked through, substantial justifications for concern about the long-run health of the primary group foundations of the modern American polity will remain.

The matter is, I believe, extremely complex. The loosening of tribal primary group bonds, for example, may be a necessary condition for the growth of personal freedom, and especially for the extension of freedom to disadvantaged minorities. Analysts of American democracy are on the verge of a valuable and invigorating debate.

I think nevertheless it is possible to conclude that by reasonably objective standards contemporary American democracy meets criteria classifying it as a vigorously functioning polyarchy, and that trends over the past thirty years or so, on most relevant counts, have shown improvement.

III

Harold Wilensky has proposed a sensible set of criteria for assessing the adequacy of contemporary policy outcomes. He has suggested that a given array of political outcomes might be regarded as unsatisfactory or at least problematic if (1) many or all other nations similarly situated displayed a different pattern of outcomes, (2) at least some U.S. political elites wanted to move toward the international norm, and (3) public opinion generally supported the indicated move. Examples would be gun control and national health insurance. They point to the strong possibility that there are organizational anomalies in the ways the United States deals with at least some sorts of regulatory affairs and issues of public expenditure as compared with the rich parliamentary democracies of Western Europe.

In fact, we all know perfectly well that the U.S. political system incorporates many features that from the standpoint of most Western democracies constitute organizational anomalies. Foremost among these is a separation of powers, the chief distinctive feature of which is not a strong president but a strong Congress. It is a common mistake in the conventional taxonomies of democratic political systems to classify the United States as an idiosyncratically successful presidential regime, amidst a rather ramshackle set of presidential systems elsewhere, to be contrasted with broadly successful parliamentary regimes.

But the point that needs to be grasped about the American political system is not that so much authoritative policymaking resides in the hands of the president but rather that so much power is held in tension and shared between president and Congress—a "separated" system, as Charles O. Jones rightly calls it, entailing multiple points of initiative and of veto. An important consequence for the making of policy is that a separated system strikes a completely different balance than parliamentary regimes between what my colleagues Bruce Cain and Nathaniel Persily call the tyranny of the majority and the tyranny of the status quo. Significant movement in public policy in a status quo-friendly system like that of the United States frequently requires a far more concentrated dose of political will, skill, and luck than in the smaller Western European democracies. But when the movement takes place, it is more likely to enjoy wide legitimacy and is less likely to be reversed.

I will not dwell on the pathologies of parliamentary regimes: insufficiently legitimate, seesaw policymaking for the majoritarian systems following the Westminster model; stasis, cycling, the tyranny of small minorities, and overreliance upon bureaucrats for the nonmajoritarian, proportional representation variant. In the United States, bureaucrats do not have the power to break stalemates between Congress and president. Rather, bargains leading to supermajorities must be sought by elected officials. Policy proposals can be successfully resisted in the intervals between elections, and elections settle less about the future course of policymaking than is true in the parliamentary democracies.

The U.S. organizational design is not to be recommended to all nations seeking a constitution. But it is reasonably well adapted to the tasks of dealing with the myriad concerns of a vast, extended republic, whose far-flung constituent parts may rightly worry about excessive governmental activity at the center adverse to their immediate interests. Thus, the size and heterogeneity, by section, occupation, generation, ethnicity, religion, and language, of the U.S. population may readily account for the existence of interests strongly supporting multiple points of veto in a constitutional design. This design, at any rate, is what the United States has.

There are added constitutional complications, notably federalism, which favors the decentralized application of policy, and the adversarial legalism that proceeds from the empowerment of judicial review inherent in a written Bill of Rights. These varied elements of constitutional design, which sustain the underlying heterogeneity of interests in a large and diverse American population, seem adequate to explain patterns of policy results differing from outcomes in smaller, more tightly organized parliamentary democracies.

Despite the drastic differences in scale between the American polity and those with which it is frequently compared, it must also be said that it is not at all uncommon for policy innovation in the United States to build on examples furnished by the smaller parliamentary democracies. Evidently observers do not find it remarkable that this should be the case, but they should. The size and demographic variety of a nation's population deeply affects its governability, especially by democratic means. Instead of marveling that the United States is not more like Norway (population 4 million, virtually all ethnic Norwegians) or the United Kingdom (with one-fourth the population of the United States, and where the Welsh, Scots, and Irish are the predominant sources of demographic and tribal diversity), observers might better focus on the remarkable fact that the United States maintains civil peace and expands civil rights even as well as it does. In this the United States is more akin to the Low Countries, with their deep and institutionalized divisions of language and religion. Characteristic American solutions to problems of civil peace in the face of diversity have differed from those of Belgium, however. They exploit the size of the nation through such devices as geographic mobility, economic expansion, and cross-cutting cleavages.

If one accepts the premise that tribalism is a human universal, then the incarceration of Japanese-Americans in World War II, the exclusion of Jews from universities and the professions in the 1920s and 1930s, the ruthless persecution of Mormons, the removal of Indian tribes, and the maintenance of a brutal, racial caste system in the pre-1960s South seem less remarkable than the eventual alleviation, reversal, or abandonment of all these social policies by the American political system. Looking, moreover, at the overall record of Western Europe during a comparable time period, it is not at all clear that despite its organizational singularities the American approach to democratic self-government suffers greatly by comparison.